THE COMPLETE

FLOWER

ARRANGER

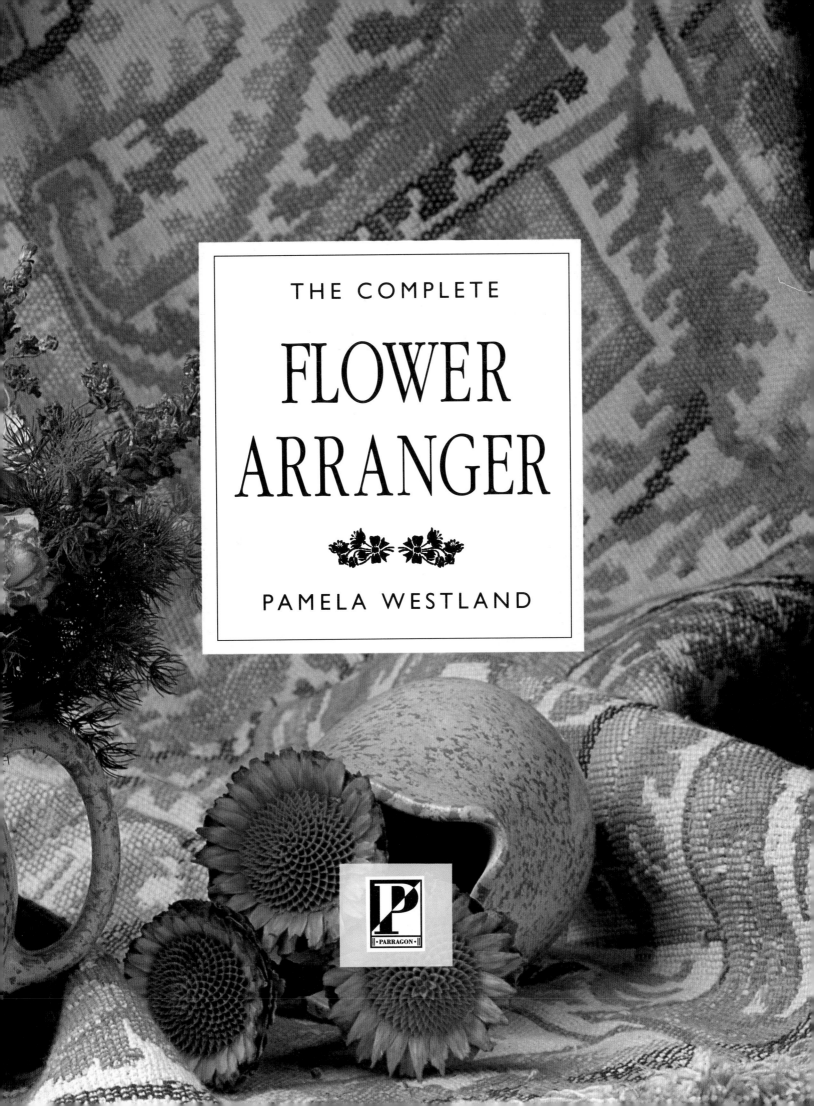

THE COMPLETE

FLOWER
ARRANGER

PAMELA WESTLAND

This edition published in 1997 by
Parragon
Units 13-17
Avonbridge Trading Estate
Atlantic Road
Avonmouth
Bristol BS11 9QD

© Anness Publishing Limited 1992

Produced by
Anness Publishing Limited
Hermes House, 88-89 Blackfriars Road,
London SE1 8HA

ISBN 0-75252-152-7 (hardback)
ISBN 0-75252-163-2 (paperback)

Publisher: Joanna Lorenz
Project Editors: Judith Simons, Lindsay Porter
Photographer: Nelson Hargreaves
Designer: Tony Paine

Printed and bound in Italy

CONTENTS

INTRODUCTION

The art of flower arranging is a decorative expression of a number of artistic skills – and you do not have to be an artist to possess them. It combines an eye for colour with an appreciation of the wide variety of textures and shapes that are to be found in flowering and foliage plants; a sense of style, whether country or classic, Oriental or modern; and a sense of artistic proportion.

Happily, these skills – almost intuitive senses – are not the exclusive prerogative of people who have spent years studying the theory of floral art and they can be readily acquired by everyone. Once you start 'thinking flowers' and explore the possibilities of both formal and informal designs, you will find inspiration in the garden or the countryside, in works of art from the Old Masters through the Impressionists to modern paintings, and in furnishing and fashion styles.

In this book, you will find reassurance, encouragement, and inspiration in the design projects which take you step-by-step through arrangements of all kinds and for all occasions, showing you the 'ingredients' you will need for each – the flowers, foliage, container, and holding materials – and then, in each series of colour photographs, the order in which to arrange them.

From the moment you gather or buy flowers from a florists' or market stall to the moment when you step back to admire your completed arrangement this book will offer you practical advice and artistic inspiration.

The first section tells you when to harvest plant materials, how to prepare them so that they will have the longest possible vase-life, and how to maintain fresh flower arrangements to keep them at their best. It shows you how to blend flower colours to compose arrangements which are bold and arresting or restrained and harmonious, and how to choose designs that will suit your own life-style. And it shows you how to put this knowledge into practice to compose 'theme' arrangements that are romantic, modern, or traditional.

The second section develops the skills a stage further and shows you how to create flower arrangements for special occasions, from church festivals to formal dinner parties, and from family weddings and anniversaries to gift-day tokens.

The third section takes an appreciative look at the many ways you can preserve the floral harvest of each season to enjoy arrangements that have an everlasting quality. Air-drying, drying in desiccants and preserving in glycerin are all techniques you can use to build up your own collection of materials to compose into hanging bunches, indoor trees, aromatic wreaths, and more traditional container arrangements. Add the traditional art of making potpourri and the childhood joy of pressing leaves and flowers and you have a range of materials to use in the infinite and fascinating variety of flowercraft.

This casual arrangement looks as if it were just picked from the garden. The holder is a florists' plastic tray fitted with soaked stem-holding foam and arranged with a vibrant mixture of dahlias, spray chrysanthemums, irises, and chincherinchee. The cascading trails of pampas grass exaggerate the horizontal line. **Above**

This midsummer cascade of wild and garden flowers is arranged in an ice bowl, the coolest of all hot-weather containers. It is made by standing a bowl inside a larger one partly filled with water, and pushing flowers into the gap. Once it is frozen, it can be kept on ice until the moment before the party and later returned to the freezer for further use. **Right**

THE ESSENTIAL
FLOWER
ARRANGER

~

Whether you choose to arrange an armful of goldenrod
and marigolds in a painted jug or a subtle harmony of
freesias and lilies in a traditional urn, every flower
arrangement you compose can be an expression of your
own artistic style. The following pages will help you
develop that style, from the moment you gather a bunch
of flowers, through the choice of container and the
appropriate holding materials, to the overall shape of
the design and the most flattering way to display it.
It also takes an appreciative look at the relationship of
plant colours and textures and explains how you can
blend them to create the most pleasing effects, and
shows you step-by-step how to achieve both classic
arrangements and more informal compositions.

A bunch of yellow daffodils bringing a welcome ray of sunshine-brightness to the breakfast table on an early spring morning; a clutch of delicate wayside flowers gathered on a summer's day; a blaze of golden, red, russet, and brown flowers and fruits, the glories of autumn; a simple jug of glowing berries and glistening evergreen leaves, the pride of winter evoking thoughts of cosy log fires and frost on the windowpanes. However they are displayed, flowers and leaves can enhance the home throughout the year.

The way flowers and foliage are arranged, either together or separately, speaks volumes about individual style, personality, and even the mood of the moment. Give ten people an identical bunch of flowers, an identical container, an option of various types of stem-holding material, and a free hand to create the arrangement of their choice, and the results would be as varied and individual as the people themselves.

One arranger may delight in placing the flowers unceremoniously in the container to give them a carefree, just-as-they-were-picked look. Another, thinking perhaps of a niche or alcove as a suitable background, may form the flowers into a gracious curve, a design with a look of classic elegance, while a third may opt for the clean, uncluttered lines of a geometric shape such as a triangle. If one of the arrangers is feeling on top of the world at the time, he or she may create an exuberant sunburst of a design, whereas someone in a tranquil and reflective mood may unwittingly express those feelings in a design that takes a compact form and suggests restraint.

Two points arise from this imaginary experiment. Firstly, a flower design should be a free expression of the arranger's individual style, just as a painting should express the way an artist sees a subject. No design is 'wrong', though some arrangements may have a better sense of balance than others – a sense that is reassuringly easy to learn and achieve.

Secondly – and this is what makes flower arranging such an infinitely absorbing pastime – with that single bunch of flowers and that one specified container it should be possible to create any number of widely different designs, from country style to classic, to suit a variety of different backgrounds, situations, and occasions.

A Matter of style

The choice of flower-arranging style, whether Oriental or traditional, elegant or romantic, is as personal as a sense of fashion, and just as rewarding to achieve. Your own instinctive style, the one that comes most readily to mind as soon as you start to put together your combination of containers, flowers, and foliage, will be influenced by your preference for colours, your normal life-style, and by the furnishings in your home. An impressive display of

An armful of spring flowers gathered straight from the garden might look like this. The design is etched with slender twigs laden with catkins. Visual weight at the base is provided by clusters of deep green ivy thick with berries. **Right**

Welcome guests with a floral arrangement on the steps or in the porch, or brighten a patio or balcony corner with a duet of garden flowers. The striped pottery container is filled with heavy and sweetly-scented bunches of white lilac and contrastingly delicate stems of deep mauve crane's-bill geranium. **Opposite**

The heavy green glass dish suggests an arrangement of waterside plants in cool colours. With the simplicity of Oriental designs, the irises and hosta – or plantain lily – leaves compose a vertical outline. The speckled glass sphere adds to the feeling of cool, clear water. **Right**

snow-white lilies and expensive roses might look somewhat out of place if you were inviting friends to an informal supper in the kitchen, whereas a group of earthenware flowerpots or decorative preserve jars topped by single mopheads of greeny-blue hydrangeas could look both interesting and arresting.

When you plan to decorate your home for a special party or decorate a church or public hall for a wedding, you will still bring your own sense of style to the occasion, adapting your preferred designs to suit the degree of

formality. If, for example, baskets brimming over with garden flowers and trailing leaves are absolutely 'you', then you can still create designs in that genre for the special day. A wide, shallow basket cascading with pastel-coloured or all-white flowers would look as delightful as any more formal arrangement on top of a pedestal in church; and a deep basket filled to the brim with zingy, vibrant blooms would be a welcoming focal point at your party, whether in the porch, the hall, the hearth, or a corner of a room.

In fact, a flower arrangement can be the focal point of any room at any time, and one which you can change at whim, particularly when you are using fresh flowers. Just by your choice of flower colour, shape, and texture, you can create the kind of highlight in your room that makes visitors exclaim and think you have completely changed the decorations. In a room principally furnished with green and white, for example, you can 'keep it cool' and create an arrangement of ice-cold lilies, cream roses, and the glossiest of deep green leaves; a study of understatement. During a more flamboyant mood you could fill a similar container – a tall, cylindrical vase spatter-painted grey and white – with a medley of orange, yellow, and pink tulips, and suddenly the flowers would light up the entire room.

Once you realize the design potential of the simplest of arrangements, you will discover the everyday world around us is full of inspiration, a powerhouse of ideas that are there to be noticed – ideas for the mix and match of colours, for the juxtaposition of contrasting textures, and for varying styles of arrangement.

It is natural, perhaps, to turn first to the great artists for inspiration in matters of both colour and style. While no one expects you slavishly to copy a medieval or modernist painting, an art gallery or even a comprehensive selection of postcards or greetings cards in a shop can not only spark off ideas, but help you to assess and develop your own floral art style.

Among the works of the Old Masters you might, with your own home in mind, care to compare the tranquil simplicity of a white bowl of arching, wax-like tulips – a graceful focal point in a largely black-and-white room scheme – with the exuberance of an urn filled to profusion with tall and slender, round and robust flowers of every shape, texture, and hue, with gleaming fruit and vegetables for good measure and – a characteristically pastoral accessory – often a bird's nest as well. A similar generosity of both flower type and colour was revived in Victorian times, and paintings of that period provide just the edge of encouragement some flower arrangers may need to experiment with garden or hothouse floral blends of predominantly pink, purple, red, and blue flowers, with roses and camellias taking pride of place.

And then there are the Impressionists, whose style is both exciting and exhilarating to recreate with flowers in the home. You may choose to set a bunch of tissue-paper-thin poppies in the palest palette of pastel colours, soft pink, creamy-white, and the barest yellow, against the

Arranged in glorious profusion in a brown glazed pot, the spring flowers compose an all-round design with more than a hint of the early Dutch style.
Below

shafts of sunlight streaking in from a window; or a large bunch of petally marigolds in almost a single plane, the flowers nestling among bright sprays of goldenrod or delicate willow leaves.

A walk in the countryside, along the coast, or in the garden can be a rewarding primary source of inspiration to flower arrangers, just as it is to artists. The way the light glances through the trees may highlight a bunch of yellowing leaves, a clutch of berries, or a handful of seedheads, and alert you to the fact that nature has much to offer, even as winter approaches. The 'Wild Look'

A basket of autumn flowers, fruits, and seedheads makes a beautiful, if transient, decoration, and looks ahead to winter arrangements with its combination of fluffy old man's beard seedheads, glossy rosehips, russety spray chrysanthemums, sedum, and Chinese lanterns (winter cherry). **Left**

arrangement, composed of materials gathered in the wild at just such a time of year and inspired by the exaggerated curve of a couple of green-going-on-yellow oak branches, was derived in that very way.

It is not only the colour, but the texture of plant materials that plays a predominant part in how a floral display is perceived. The autumnal basket display mentioned above takes a leaf from nature's book and sets shiny-bright berries, which represent only a minimal proportion of the design as a whole, against matt textures and spiky outlines. The prominence of the berries has been assured because they are surrounded, as they may be in the wild, by the distinctly no-gloss element of old man's beard (*Clematis vitalba, C. virginiana*), the almost woody appearance of poppy seedheads, and the spiky spires of wheat.

Late in the season, a rose bush in the wild or in the garden creates a contrast of textures which can bring vibrant visual rewards indoors. As the rosehips ripen and glisten around it, a single rose, evocatively perceived as the last rose of summer, seems all the more romantic and delicate by comparison, and, in their turn, the berries seem even brighter and glossier.

This juxtaposition of shiny and matt, sparkling and velvety textures can be carried out to rewarding effect in floral displays of all kinds. Create the illusion of sidelighting, of sun shafts or lamplight, in a simple way by arranging glossy-petalled flowers such as lilies on one side of a container, and matt ones, maybe spider chrysanthemums, on the other. In a dark corner of a room, you can create the illusion of more light than there is by choosing the sunniest flowers and foliage available.

To create the impression of greater depth in an arrangement and impart a three-dimensional effect, position matt materials towards the back and into the centre, where they will be seen in partial shadow, and allow the shiny ones to come forward and steal the limelight.

In a garden or the countryside, you might notice the made-for-each-other pairing of glossy ivy leaves or wild roses entwined around the craggy bark of a tree, or on a seashore, the heightened beauty of delicate wild lupins (lupines) outlined against a breakwater. In this way, country and seashore walks can become treasure hunts: pieces of craggy wood are among the most precious *objets trouvés*, the craggier and more lichen-covered or salt-washed the better. Failing a lucky find of a piece of fallen tree or shapely driftwood, you can buy interesting specimens in florists' shops.

An angular piece of vinewood can become the 'tree' under which a drift of pale daffodils is arranged amid a mossy ground cover – an unusual interpretation of an Easter arrangement for a church. A sinuous piece of gnarled wood can simulate a fallen log and become a perfect foil, by virtue of the textural contrast, to clutches of delicate flowers; while knobbly twigs snapped off or fallen from an apple tree can create striking outlines and a natural look in otherwise conventional designs.

SHADES AND HUES

If on the spur of the moment you treat yourself to a few bunches of flowers from a market stall, or pause to admire a flower-filled garden, you will most certainly be influenced by colour, by the powerful impact of buckets of flowers spilling onto the pavement, or by the more considered effect of a formally maintained garden.

Setting aside the occasional impulse purchase, your choice of flowers for the home will usually take into

An uncluttered look for a kitchen, a study in cool greens and creams. The double narcissus are arranged with sprays of mimosa in bud and variegated ivy in an oval basket-weave container. **Above**

The warm glow of winter is exemplified by this gleaming leaf and berry arrangement in an old beer stein. The holly and ivy leaves look even more glossy when they are contrasted with matt foliage, in this case cypress and furry-leaved ballota. **Left**

Accessories can form a key element in still-life groups or even, as here, inspire the composition of the arrangement. The flowering currant, echoing the pattern of the potpourri cushion, forms an irregular triangle with bi-coloured tulips. **Right**

CHOOSING HUES

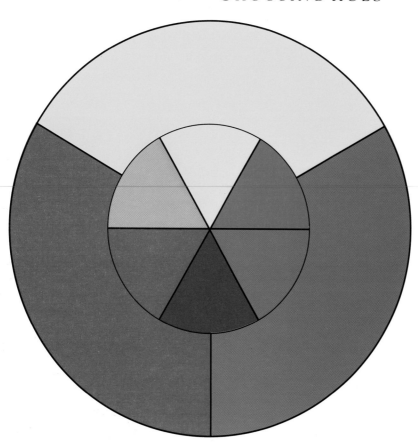

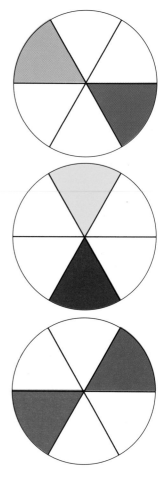

account your furnishings, the background against which they will be seen, and the effect you wish to create. A bunch of golden-yellow flowers, high on the list of impulse buys since yellow is considered a 'happy' colour, can work wonders in brightening a dull day. But, perhaps surprisingly, it is not just the colour of the flowers themselves that creates a vibrant and vigorous or calm and composed effect, but the interplay of flower and background colour together.

That bunch of sunshine-yellow daffodils, with all its cheering propensities, would have a limited impact in design terms if placed against an orange curtain or a window framing an expanse of green lawn. Move it to a table covered with a red or blue cloth, and the yellow seems to intensify; place it where the flowers are viewed against mauve, and they positively glow.

Take, as another example, a bunch of bright red flowers, scarlet dahlias, for instance, and you might think that, no matter what the furnishing scheme, they would pack the most powerful colour punch possible. They would, if placed against green, but their brilliance would be visually diluted if moved in front of an orange wall or a mauve curtain. And so the message is clear: if you want to create a real, visual, impression with a gift of red roses, surround them with green foliage, or tie them with a big green ribbon bow.

The cause of this effect is most readily understood by reference to what is known as a colour wheel, representing the sequence of colours as they are seen in the rainbow, and as they relate to one another. The theory of the use of colour can help you to choose flowers in the single colour most likely to create a vibrant or restrained effect in any part of the home, and to select floral blends that harmonize or perfectly complement each other.

The wheel is divided into six segments. Each of the alternate sections is made up of the three primary colours: red, blue, and yellow. Between those are the secondary colours, the ones which result from mixing the primaries: mauve by blending red and blue, green derived from blue and yellow, and orange resulting from a red and yellow

Familiarity with the colour wheel will help you to choose flower colours to create a particular effect. The large wheel is divided into six sections, showing the primaries – red, yellow, and blue – and the colours derived from mixing them. The smaller colour wheels illustrate the complementary colours – those opposite one another on the wheel. Used together, complementary colours are seen to best advantage.
Opposite

Flowers for a garden room or working conservatory can have a high degree of informality. Arranged in a pottery watering-can, the orange marigolds and nasturtiums contrast with the blue love-in-a-mist and pansies to create a complementary scheme. **Below**

blue jug with a towering partnership of bright orange Chinese lanterns (winter cherry), fresh or dried, midnight-blue larkspur, and misty-blue sea holly; combine blue iris in a springtime group with marmalade-orange narcissus and tulips; or, later in the year, mix blue Michaelmas daisies with rusty chrysanthemums and autumn leaves in a copper jug.

The interpretation of this complementary-colour pairing, the 'Complete Harmony' arrangement, was inspired by a modern oil painting, and grew from there. Not everyone happens to have containers in just the right colours for a scheme: for this arrangement two stone mustard jars were drizzle-painted and filled with lilies, larkspur, iris and anemones, with a cluster of pyracantha (firethorn) berries for extra glow and contrasting texture.

The equally vibrant mauve-and-yellow partnership could be interpreted in a variety of moods; with the pretty springtime pairing of pale primroses and deep purple

mix. To take the illustration a stage further, each segment may be divided into sections to represent the strength of the colour, from the deepest shades when the colour is mixed with black, to the palest pastel tints when it is blended with white in varying degrees. With this colour tool, you can evaluate the effect each colour has on its neighbour, and the effect each flower or group of flowers would have on its companions in an arrangement.

To put the theory to the test, there is no need to gather a basketful of flowers in all colours of the rainbow, or to make a lavish experimental purchase at the florists . Cut out coloured blocks from a magazine or use small paint samples, shuffling them into various pairings and groups – deepest violet with palest blue, a pleasant harmony; pale pink with bright orange, warm but not particularly strident; bright blue with brilliant orange, an exercise in going for bold.

COMPLEMENTARY HUES

When two colours that oppose each other on the wheel are used together, in full strength, the outlook is dazzling: primary blue and secondary orange; primary yellow and secondary mauve; primary red and secondary green. These pairings, which illustrate the attraction of colour opposites and speak volumes in impact terms, are known as complementary, or contrasting.

To take the blue-and-orange combination as an exercise in scene-stealing arrangements, you could fill a tall,

YULETIDE DISPLAYS

Sometimes it may be a favourite container, sometimes a particular background, sometimes the seasonal availability of the plant materials, or sometimes tradition that suggests arrangements in certain colour pairings. Can it be coincidence or is it simply luck that at Christmastime both tradition and the range of plant materials available to us – all the glowing tints and shades of evergreens and the contrasting brightness of their berries – lead us to deck our homes in the complementary-colour pairing of red and green?

In celebration of the festival, you may choose to arrange a few sprays of variegated leaves and scarlet berries in a still-life group with a trio of red candles; combine the softness of a grey-green plant such as ballota with glossy green ivy and holly; or gather together the brightest flowers of the season, be they poinsettia, carnations, or anemones, in a jade-green jug or a bright red biscuit or cookie tin. Whatever your choice, you can be sure that you have both tradition and colour balance on your side.

A green and white arrangement looks suitably seasonal at Christmas, an echo of frost and snow covering the evergreens outside. The table design, which combines white freesias, roses, and spray carnations with holly and snowberries, is tied with green ribbons. **Left**

A host of orange marigolds combined with soft, fluffy sprays of goldenrod creates a bright and casual composition in colours which are adjacent on the colour wheel. This simple grouping forms a perfect visual link between the home and the garden, and would strike a welcoming note on the breakfast table. **Right**

violets arranged in bunches in a wooden basket. You could gather the flowers into a posy, tie the stems with a handful of raffia, and place them in a mauve or yellow container or, for a touch more originality, in a scooped-out lemon fitted with a small water-holding container. This is similar to what has been done in the 'Perfect Complement' arrangement. The container, a hollowed-out melon shell, gave the lead for the colour-coordinated scheme, a luxuriant complement of orchids and carnations together with fluffy mimosa, high-sheen lilies, and soft-petalled roses.

ADJACENT SHADES

At the other end of the impact scale are the colour pairings, descriptively termed adjacent, that are next to each other on the colour wheel and considered to be harmonious, even restrained. Red and mauve, mauve and blue, and so on around the wheel indicate the pairings or groupings that are closely related. This harmony is perfectly illustrated by a cluster of anemones, all the reds, mauves, and blues blending together, with each colour playing an equal part in the whole arrangement; or, in a sunnier vein, by a bunch of dahlias in brilliant orange, yellow, and red, arranged for the greatest impact in a black container.

ALTERNATE SHADES

The third group of colour pairings, the alternates – those that are one place away from each other on the wheel – are considered more difficult to use with ease in floral designs; this applies especially to full-strength red and yellow, orange and mauve. But there are times when you may want an arrangement which positively commands attention in colour terms. The occasion may arise at the height of summer, when a floral display for a party in the garden has to compete with the deep blue of the sky and the brilliance of the sun; at the New Year, when everyone is in party mood and the flowers have to match it; or, indeed, at any large informal gathering, when an arrangement has to be seen across a crowded room. At such times a basket painted deep purple and filled with a mass of purple and lemon-yellow statice, or a red enamel container burgeoning with scarlet and yellow lilies could perfectly capture the mood of the moment.

MAKING ROOM

Every room in the home, almost every nook and cranny, can be greatly enhanced from time to time by a flower arrangement, however fleeting or modest it may be. The dining room and living room are 'naturals' for floral decorations, especially when you are entertaining friends, but other areas can be made more welcoming or relaxing just by the thoughtful addition of flowers.

Think first of the entrance, the porch or hall. This is the area that gives visitors their first impression of your home; flowers will make sure it is a welcoming one.

At Christmastime and, increasingly, at other seasonal festivals, it is the custom to welcome visitors to our homes with an evergreen or floral wreath on the door: a verdant hoop of holly and ivy in winter, or a ring of fresh flowers in all colours of the rainbow at Easter or in the height of summer. But there is no need to restrict this floral welcome to the holidays. It is cheering to see an informal grouping of bright blooms on a porch at any time of year. Big is beautiful in this type of setting, and a basket or even a lightly disguised bucket of the cheapest flowers of the season strikes a note of welcome. As a more permanent feature, a display of foliage and flowering houseplants can be placed to good effect, well protected from the elements, with perhaps a small stepladder standing in for the more formal *étagère*.

A front-facing windowsill can also take on the welcoming role, with an 'all-round' arrangement that looks equally good from both inside and outside the home. Here, too, flower colours should be bold rather than restrained. Dried flowers can be a good choice. A dried arrangement of mixed foliage, peonies, roses, and sea lavender colour-coordinated to the room scheme would offer a bright hello.

For a hall or a narrow passage, place an impulse buy of bunches of spring or summer flowers, or a more permanent display of dried grasses, cereals, and seedheads colour-spiked with preserved berries and Chinese lanterns (winter cherry).

When space is of the essence, flowers can cheerfully take to the walls. Junk shops and flea markets are good sources of wall vases dating from the 1930s and 1940s, shell-shaped or fan-shaped, pastel or brilliantly coloured, and purpose-made for a narrow setting such as a hall or passage. For an ever-changing display, fit a vase with soaked foam, arrange long trails of evergreen foliage – eucalyptus would be perfectly in keeping – and ring the

Think of the glorious colours and shapes that crowd a well-stocked herbaceous border. Here they are, in a country-style arrangement that would look good on a patio, porch, or hearth. From the brilliant red of the valerian and pyrethrums, through the mauve of the delphiniums and Canterbury bells to the blue cornflowers, the colours are adjacent to each other on the colour wheel and form a harmonious group. **Below**

NEW CONTAINERS FOR OLD

No matter how many containers you have, there always comes a time when you long for one in a particular colour to harmonize with a scheme you have in mind. You might have a woven rug hanging as a wall covering and want to use it as a background for flowers, yet all your vases, teapots, milk jugs, and salad bowls are too strident. You might have redecorated a room and want to celebrate with flowers, yet none of your favourite containers looks exactly right. Or you may be a compulsive bargain hunter, unable to resist a tempting buy in junk shops and flea markets. If this is the case, you are likely to have a cupboard full of items in all shapes and sizes, but not necessarily tailor-made for your home.

A pot or two of paint can change all that. You may have some left over from decorating, or you can now buy sample pots, complete with mini brush, in a wide range of colours – just the thing for artistic experimentation.

Before you start, thoroughly wash and dry the article – a clean, dry surface is essential – and cover every surface within range with newspaper.

The easiest way to paint a cylindrical glass vase, for example, is to hold it upside-down on a length of cane. In that way you do not have to touch it. Give it an even coat of paint in one colour, and

A selection of containers including jugs, vases, mugs, beakers, coffee and teapots, a used food can, and a basket, which are suitable for arranging both fresh flowers (with a waterproof liner where appropriate) and dried plant materials. **Left**

A selection of baskets and wooden boards which may be used as containers and bases for arrangements of both fresh flowers and dried plant materials. **Below**

leave it to dry thoroughly. For a spattered look dip an old toothbrush or paintbrush into a saucer of paint in a second colour. Take care not to overload the brush, and run your thumb or a ruler along the bristles to produce a fine spray of droplets. The container should look as if it has been splashed by coloured rain. If you are not confident of your painting technique, experiment first on a piece of paper until you achieve an even, but not too even, finish. You can build up the colour, and your confidence, by adding a third and even a fourth colour. In a modern setting or for a young person's room, it may be a case of the more the merrier.

For a sponged finish, apply the second colour in blotches and smudge them with a small rolled-up ball of plastic sponge or, for a softer look, use a piece of marine sponge.

Random stripes are child's play; you boldly draw the brush down or around the painted container to streak it with a contrasting colour. If you want to make the stripes even, as they are in many beautiful Art Deco pieces, mask those areas not to be painted with adhesive or masking tape, and paint between the lines. When that coat has dried, remove the tape and, if you wish, mask other areas.

It is a fascinating art form, and one with endless possibilities. You can mask painted areas by painting them with gum arabic, which will cause the next layer you apply to peel or crackle; or streak a thick layer of paint by running a comb through it. There is no end of ways to transform a dowdy wine carafe, a faded jug or a hideous teapot into the vase of the moment.

changes with a weekly bunch of daffodils, anemones, or any other seasonal flowers. For a more permanent display you could arrange a generous fan shape or an impressive cascade of dried flowers and preserved foliage in colours to complement the wall covering. A more countrified look would have a wall basket filled to overflowing with dried cereals and a kaleidoscope of strawflowers. Baskets come from all over the world and offer a wide choice of styles, from natural or bleached willow to plaited stems and woven fern leaves.

Other ideas tailor-made for no-space situations include floral wreaths of all kinds, and hanging posies or bunches of dried flowers. A stem wreath from the florist can be transformed in moments by sticking on a polka-dot look of perky pink strawflowers. A hanging bunch can be as simple as you please. Just three handfuls of dried statice in toning colours, tied with raffia, is enough to spell a warm welcome.

FLORAL DISPLAYS THROUGHOUT THE HOME

Just as each room in the house serves a different function, so different floral displays in appropriate styles will enhance their environment – cool and reflective for a bedroom or study, bright and cheerful for a busy kitchen, or elegant and sophisticated for a formal dining room. There are no hard and fast rules, but the following suggestions may help you to assess your own surroundings.

IN THE DINING ROOM

The dining room has a high profile in flower arranging terms, since it becomes the centre stage whenever the family gathers for a leisurely meal – at Sunday lunchtime, perhaps – or when entertaining friends. At other times, it may have long periods of inactivity. Even so, it is a good idea to have an eye-catching dried-flower arrangement on the dining table or a side table, so that the room always has a welcoming and lived-in look, and is permanently at the ready for unexpected guests.

If you have more than one arrangement in the room – there may be one on the table, a sideboard, and a table by the window – it is a good idea to compose them with a linking theme. It could be that the flowers on the sideboard would be seen against a pale-coloured wall and those on the table against dark wood, or that the wallcovering is heavily patterned and the tablecloth plain, so designs with an identical colour match would not be in keeping. Even so, it is easier on the eye if the

arrangements have a common bond. Bridge the light and dark background gap by choosing similar flowers, but in different colours: deep-pink Peruvian lilies, for example, in one case and the palest of pinks in another. Outline a sideboard arrangement with a distinguishing frame of foliage, or choose flowers in a single colour and type that will be seen in high relief against the most competitive of backgrounds. A tall pitcher of white iris on the sideboard could be interpreted by floating similar flowers in a glass bowl on the dining table, by placing a single flower in a specimen vase at each place setting, or by blending white iris, in a long, low arrangement with anemones or roses, for example.

When planning the arrangements, take into account the impact factor. Make sure at least one arrangement is in the line of vision as guests come into the room; that a sideboard arrangement is tall enough – though not over-whelmingly so – to be in full view of at least some of the guests once they are seated; and that any arrangement on a low table really does look its best when seen from above, with a bird's-eye view. Dome shapes, low pyramids, and both regular and irregular all-round shapes come into this last category.

IN THE LIVING ROOM

Similar general criteria apply to flower arrangements for a sitting or living room. You can compose the most delight-ful design imaginable, but if it is placed on a low table behind the sofa, the arrangement is unlikely to receive the attention it deserves.

If there is a fireplace, then it is normally the focal point of the room, and can remain so even when a fire is not lit. The well of the fireplace forms a dramatic arch for a flamboyant arrangement of seasonal plant materials chosen according to the colour and texture of the fire-place surround: a large earthenware jug of just-opening horse-chestnut buds in spring, a cool blend of blues and greens in summer, and the more evocative hues of fiery red, orange, and yellow as winter approaches.

A wide windowsill or a table in front of the window can provide a transition between the room and the garden or street outside, and go a long way towards creating a relaxing and pleasant environment. You can use the space to mask an uninspiring view or block out the grey sky by composing a large-scale but lightweight arrangement, one which draws a natural veil over the world outside yet

A formal design for a table centre, this pyramid shape is outlined with yellow and orange montbretia stems and – unusually – filled in with rounded flowers of equal size, which include zinnias, spray carnations, and roses. **Opposite**

The black arched fireplace makes a dramatic backdrop for an elegant floral display in a cream pottery container. Foxgloves and briar roses etch in the outlines, pale pink peonies form the focal point, and phlox and aquilegia are used as filler material. **Right**

allows the light to filter through. In summer, especially if the window faces south, fresh flowers are vulnerable and will fade quickly. In these circumstances, achieve the best of both worlds and choose the brightest and boldest of containers to display sun-bleached seedheads; fill a large white jug with a burst of fresh or dried gypsophila and strawflowers; pack a basket full of oats and decorative grasses, and wrap it with a brightly-coloured paper ribbon bow; or go for the leafy look, and arrange arching stems of translucent, dramatically back-lit foliage.

In a different vein, and especially when the window overlooks a garden, a flower arrangement can link the two elements, reinforcing the colour of the flowers outside or adding brightness where it is lacking. A long, low flower arrangement on a windowsill, too low to catch the rays of the sun, can be as pleasing and restful as a thickly planted flowerbed outside the window.

While flowers in the fireplace and at the window are for shared enjoyment, give a special, individual pleasure to family and friends by placing individual arrangements

close to separate seating areas – the nicest possible way to make someone feel pampered. It could be a sweetly scented posy of herbs and garden flowers beside Granny's favourite chair, a bowl of purple and yellow pansies glowing beneath a reading lamp, a jug of daisies to provide relaxation and inspiration in an area set aside for home-work, or a single favourite flower in a vase by your own armchair or work area.

IN THE BEDROOM

Flower arrangements for a bedroom or guest room are unashamed tokens of indulgence, and should be both romantic and restful. Choose pastel colours or the 'cool' shades of blue, mauve, and green in preference to the more strident hues of full-strength red and yellow, and avoid flowers that are too heavily scented. Hyacinths or an over-abundance of freesias, for example, can give some people a headache. Perhaps 'arrangement' is too specific a term where bedroom flowers are concerned. Choose the prettiest jug you can find, and fill it with a handful of fully opened roses or a nosegay of roses, lilies, and larkspur in muted colours. Arrange a posy ring for a dressing table with spray carnations and daisy chrysanthemums in apri-cot and peach tints, or compose a miniature group of moody blues with forget-me-nots and cornflowers tumb-ling over the side of a blue glass pitcher.

A jug and bowl set, in the Victorian tradition, is placed where it will be highlighted by the early morning sun. The casual arrangement of partly-opened roses, larkspur, spray carnations, and goldenrod has an air of romance, and is enhanced by a subtle aroma. **Above**

Enamelware of all kinds makes inexpensive and appropriate containers for kitchen displays. In this group a red jug blends perfectly with a bunch of scarlet field poppies and its companion, a small saucepan, contrasts vividly with the snow-white feverfew. **Left**

Flowers for a child's room should be bright, cheerful, and sturdy. A colourful jug of reassuringly stable proportions holds short sprays of garden flowers in paintbox colours. It is a good idea to encourage children to take pride in the flowers by topping up the vase water and cutting off fading blooms. **Opposite**

Old-fashioned roses can be at their most appealing when they display every curling petal. In this country-style group they are contrasted with other summer-garden flowers from pale pink to bright red. The marigolds provide sharp highlights. **Left**

Tempting as it may be in view of their longevity, arranging dried flowers for a bathroom breaks all the rules about displaying them in a dry, airy place, so it is unwise to think of a design as a permanent fixture. Choose, again, from the most good-tempered examples, which include all the everlastings – strawflowers, rhodanthe, and acroclinium – statice, honesty, Chinese lanterns (winter cherry), and other seedheads. Or protect more delicate flowers under glass: an arrangement composed in dry foam on a board and covered with a glass dome – a modern cheese dish or an upturned preserve jar – would satisfy both aesthetic and practical considerations.

IN THE KITCHEN

Kitchens, too, are subject to rapid changes of temperature and, to a lesser extent, humidity, so many of the same ground rules apply. Casual floral compositions seem most likely to induce a feeling of calm composure. A jug of marigolds on the kitchen table signals a cheery early-morning greeting; a pot of herbs on the windowsill has both decorative and culinary properties; and a hanging basket of foliage plants, or grains and grasses lifts floral decor to a high level. Together, they might be all it takes to turn a business-like unit into a cosy kitchen.

SETTING THE SCENE

Certain rooms in the home, and the way each is furnished, may suggest a specific theme or style of arrangement: a romantic look for flowers in the bedroom, a country look in a farmhouse-style kitchen, a traditional approach in a more formal sitting or living room, and so on. But this is not to say that all arrangements for a kitchen should stop short at placing a bunch of daffodils in a honey pot, or all arrangements for a living room should have an authenticity based on years of tradition. There is plenty of scope to experiment with each style, adapt it to your own preferences, and present it in a way that uniquely reflects your personality.

IN THE BATHROOM

Bathrooms seem to fall into two categories: those in which everyone is always in a rush, and those that are a haven in which to relax. Make your choice of flower colours accordingly, but in either case take account of the likely temperature and humidity changes, and choose the sturdiest and most long-lasting of blooms. Among fresh flowers, these include chrysanthemums of all kinds (the white daisy and spider types look especially good in a bathroom), marigolds, carnations, spray carnations, lilies, and tulips. Containers with a hint of sparkle seem most appropriate to these surroundings: jugs, bottles, bowls, and beakers of clear, frosted or coloured glass used, if need be, with glass marbles or granite chippings to hold the stems; large shells fitted with soaked foam, and cascading with grey-green foliage and trailing flower stems; or cosmetic jars and pots of all kinds, the more luxurious-looking the better.

COUNTRY-STYLE FLOWERS

It may be that country-style arrangements are the ones most likely to have your personal imprint. This casual style of arrangement is, in fact, a good stepping-stone to the accomplishment of other designs, since it calls for the minimum of special materials – stem-holding aids and so forth – and is not confined by any mathematical principles, as some formal arrangements are.

Think of the countryside, and the images that spring to mind: fields of corn and bright red poppies; misty-blue drifts of borage and linseed (flaxseed), a wave of cultivated blue flowers; patchwork fields illuminating the landscape with brilliant yellow mustard or rapeseed; bluebell woods streaked with pale shafts of light; or meadows dappled with flowers in all the pastel tints of the spectrum. You may envisage a country garden, the beds a palette of deep blue delphiniums and anemones, sunbright marigolds and stately white lilies.

Whatever your idea of the countryside, you can interpret it in many evocative ways. A white pottery jug filled with wheat and arranged as a group with a family of maize or cornhusk dolls is undeniably country-style, as is a basket of wildflowers, perhaps buttercups, daisies, and Queen Anne's lace. Or you may want to set out a blue and

Crimson, ruby, scarlet, pastel pink – all appear in this countrified study in red and white. The flower shapes contrast well, from the full-petalled peony at the heart of the design to the lupin (lupine) and twisted stems of wild rose at the sides. **Above**

The citrus colours of the nasturtiums, marigolds, and carnations form a harmonious group, with orange, yellow, and the green of the wispy lamium leaves neighbours on the colour wheel. **Left**

white pitcher of hawthorn branches and perennial cornflowers, delightfully aromatic into the bargain; or a teapot filled with a blend of herbs – mint and marjoram, borage and balm, fennel and feverfew; or a stone pot of herbaceous flowers in shades of red through mauve to blue, pyrethrums, sweet williams and Canterbury bells among them; or even a small, round loaf of crusty bread, hollowed in the centre, baked dry, and filled (a hidden, water-holding container inside) with marigolds and lilies.

Grouping flowers together in an arrangement, type by type, is country-style, too – a sympathetic interpretation of the way they grow in fields or densely planted patches. The 'Country Style' project illustrates this perfectly: huge orange marigolds gleam like suns against a cluster of delphinium, and stems of scarlet plume (*Euphorbia fulgens*), a Mexican plant, form arches over the rim of the jug, like a tree shading a border.

Where containers are concerned, for country read casual – pottery jugs, pottery and woven baskets, blue and white china, pottery teapots, stone pots, even rustic loaves of bread. They all help to set the scene, and contribute to the pastoral look of the arrangements. Other evocative container possibilities include a collection of preserve jars, each filled with a single flower type, or a mixture, and the whole arranged as a group; various food containers, from a colourfully labelled vegetable can trailing yellow courgette (zucchini) flowers and yellow and white deadnettles, to a colourful candy packet fitted with a water glass and a cargo of flowers in vibrant hues; wooden boxes, from seed trays piled enticingly with russet-coloured fruits and flowers, to shallow date boxes fitted with plastic trays and floating with flower heads and leaves. Earthenware flowerpots are very much country-style, and can carry everything from a large single flower

A natural container for a farmhouse setting – the loaf is hollowed out and the shell baked until it is dry. It is then fitted with a liner and soaked foam and filled with a flourish of flowers in sunshine colours – carnations, marigolds, Peruvian lilies, and marjoram. **Opposite**

Brought in from the wild – the blue and white ginger jar is filled to overflowing with branches of aromatic white blackthorn blossom and perennial cornflowers, a casual arrangement suitable for a kitchen. **Left**

A large seashell makes an elegant flower holder. Here, it is arranged with pinks and everlasting sweet pea which compose an unequal triangle. The two smaller shells are used as accessories, their craggy surfaces contrasting strikingly with the mother-of-pearl appearance of the container.
Right

Blue and white jugs evoke the country; so does lady's mantle, the delicate lime-green border flower in this arrangement. The other flower colours are dramatically separated, with orange and red nasturtiums on one side, and mauve scabious and pansies on the other.
Opposite

to a nosegay of herbs, as can enamelware of all kinds, in paintbox colours. Fill a red coffee pot with scarlet poppies, another with bunches of snow-white feverfew, and a citrus yellow pot with contrastingly pale everlastings; or look to the colour wheel for inspiration, for mix-and-match alternatives and complementary pairings.

A Touch of romance

In a romantic mood, flowers can go a long way towards reviving treasured memories, and even creating a few new ones. Think of romance and flowers, and the majority of us think of roses: lovely, wild roses rambling over grassy verges; full-blown, soft-petalled roses; the deep red rosebuds that since Victorian times and beyond have symbolized true love.

If you are arranging flowers for a dinner *à deux*, your choice might well be roses. Place a glass bowl of peach- and apricot-hued roses beneath the soft glow of lamplight, where the glass will glisten and the rose petals seem more velvety than ever; place a vase of roses close to an open window so their heady scent will seem to waft in from an expansive rose garden; blend fulsome roses with dainty sprays of stephanotis, with pale green orchid buds, or, for a look of youthful innocence, daisy-like marguerites.

Arrange a basket of open roses with a cloud of lady's mantle, like a floral veil in the palest of greens, or, more conventionally, with pure white gypsophila. Give your romantic arrangement a pronounced countryside note by clustering a bunch of wild pink and white single roses or American pillar roses with the sharp contrasting green of wild spurge (*Euphorbia*) and sprays of pink, red or white campion. Place a handful of pale pink roses in a clear blue glass jug, and position them so they are partially hidden by the edge of a lace curtain.

If roses don't suit your mood, create romantic floral cameos in shades of midnight-blue and dusky pink: a collection of blue glass bottles, each holding a handful of cornflowers; a pink-painted teapot arranged with a gentle dome of trailing anemones; or a pink pottery vase tied around with satin ribbons and filled with a posy-style bunch of pink and blue poppies.

Baskets, especially if you line or trim them with lace or paper doilies, have an air of romance, as do coloured glass jugs, vases, drinking glasses, or *epergnes*. Shells are a gift in this design concept. To create a still-life group in this vein – and without a shell large enough to hold flowers – you could arrange pink through cream to white roses and ranunculus with sea lavender in a plain glass vase, entwine it with an inexpensive rope of pearl beads, and scatter a few seashells beside it.

Classic styling

Containers must be chosen with more specific attention to detail when selected for a floral design with a classic quality. It may be that a collection of flowers – roses, delphiniums, and ranunculus, say – arranged in a basket or shell evokes the countryside or romance, but arrange them in a blue and gold urn and, as long as certain guidelines are observed, the design becomes classic.

We have history to thank for this concept, dating back from the time of the Ancient Egyptians, who designed urns, vases, and other containers especially for flowers, and decorated them with flower and garland motifs; and the Ancient Greeks and Romans, who used flowers in lavish profusion at all their religious and public ceremonies.

Container shapes that originated in Egypt have been handed down to us virtually unchanged through the centuries. A deep bowl on a raised foot; a two-handled urn; a pottery fruit bowl with a decorative rim and intricate handles; a bulbous stone pot glazed in deep jewel colours with perhaps a hint of gilding; thick crystal urns in sizes from minute to massive; a tall tapered vase in jet black – these and other similar shapes have a long tradition and a thorough pedigree.

When making use of these wide-necked containers, it is often necessary to use some form of stem-holding material – either crumpled wire netting or absorbent foam – which is an aid to design unavailable in early times. (The use of these mechanics is dealt with here, and they are used in many of the projects that follow.) Such stem-holding material enables you to angle stems to slope downwards, to place others horizontally, and to create specific geometric and curved shapes.

These styles are refinements of the more free-style classic arrangements, and may be composed in a wide variety of containers. A horizontal design in a shallow rectangular box or basket, a vertical design following the lines of a tall blue and white vase, and a diagonal shape forming a rakish angle on a painted wine carafe are examples of the wide divergence of styles and the containers that suit them.

While it may be amusing to place a large mophead hydrangea in a flowerpot or jam jar, and admire its unconventionality and interesting textural contrast, such disregard of the proportion of the plant material is out of the question in a classic arrangement of any kind.

A ratio of 1½:1, plant material to container height or width, is considered the minimum to achieve a good balance in formal arrangements and more particularly in competition or exhibition displays. In practice this means that in an upright arrangement, a tall triangle or vertical composition for example, the height of the main, central stem should be at least 1½ times the height of the container. In more showy displays composed for formal occasions in a church or public hall, this proportion can be considerably greater.

A similar principle applies, but is turned on its side, in relation to horizontal arrangements. In this case, the length of each of the major side stems – a slender branch of broom or a daffodil bud, say – should be at least 1½ times the width of the container, or the base on which it stands if that forms an integral part of the design.

Although this may sound dauntingly mathematical, this ratio of plant materials to container measurement is

The tall, elegant lines of the vase are extended in this upright arrangement of cuckoo-pint leaves and spider chrysanthemums. The raised focal point is composed of bluebells and grape hyacinth (Muscari). **Right**

A springtime pyramid of wallflowers, cowslips, and primulas is arranged in an old pewter inkwell and forms part of a desk-top group. **Left**

so easy on the eye and looks so natural, that many flower arrangers, even those just beginning to practise the art, find they have been using it without noticing. If you do want to check your own ability to judge the proportion by eye, measure the central side stems before cutting them, and you will soon find you no longer need to do so.

While proportion is a key factor in classic flower arrangements, it is not the whole story. Both the colour and shape of the plant materials and the way in which they are placed play an important part in the balance of a design. In general, the materials with the most slender outlines are positioned where they will form the tip or circumference of an arrangement: stems of ballota or willow etching in the points of a geometric shape; iris buds with their pencil-point shapes outlining a ring around a full, round traditional design; or the fine lines of broom tapering at the tips of a classic curve. Materials that are visual middleweights such as Peruvian lilies, gently opening rosebuds, or ranunculus, occupy the middle ground in an arrangement; while the most fully-rounded materials – carnations, peonies, or gerberas, and large ivy or geranium leaves, for example – or those in the darkest shades are placed at the base or heart of a design, where they will give it stability and comprise the focal

point. This is because flowers in the darkest shades seem far heavier and larger than those of similar size in middle pastel tones. To prove it, try arranging a bowl of mixed dahlias, with deep purple ones at the top and pale apricot ones at the base. Step back to review your handiwork, and the purple ones will look as if they are about to crash through the roof!

ORIENTAL PRINCIPLES

Many styles considered both classic and elegant today have elements that originated in Ancient China, where floral art began. The principles of proportion and colour balance may be said to stem from the Chinese study of the line, form, colour, and texture of each plant species, while the use in many classic designs of three flowers or leaves to form the focal point of an arrangement can be traced back to the significance of this number in Chinese floral compositions.

In Oriental philosophies it is considered that one line is symbolic, two lines are harmonious, and three represent fulfilment. Western flower arrangers, without necessarily being aware of this Oriental significance, may find that while two stems of waxy white lilies in a specimen vase might look sparse and four seem crowded, three stems strike a perfect balance. Whereas two bamboo-stem vases of foliage and flowers look incomplete, three comprise a well-balanced still-life group.

Containers used in Chinese floral compositions are often beautiful and ornate works of art, hand-painted porcelain vases, glass in jewel-bright colours, and lacquer boxes among them. Such *objets* are perfectly complemented by a minimum of plant material, which may be three arching stems of plum blossom, a cluster of deep red camellias, or a trio of white chrysanthemums. This last flower is a favourite in Chinese floral art since it symbolizes innocence and purity.

A cauldron of flowers from all seasons emphasizes the wonderful variety of plant shapes and textures, from the arching stems of red euphorbia to the petally, fully-opened roses; from the trumpet shapes of freesia and Peruvian lily to the round mophead hydrangea.
Opposite

Japanese floral art, known as *ikebana* (meaning beautiful flower arrangement), evolved from the Chinese form in the sixth century, and here, too, the use of three elements has deep significance representing heaven, man, and earth. Japanese art, which would take a lifetime to study in detail, places strong emphasis on the creation of harmonious proportion and the achievement of graceful line and movement, and calls for precise placement of each individual element. To achieve this rhythm and balance a wide variety of materials is used, but sparingly: not only branches, flowers, and driftwood, but spirals of wood shavings, twisted and angular wires, rocks, stones, and even pieces of sculpture.

The economic use of natural and man-made materials also characterizes many designs in the modern idiom, which include free-form and abstract designs, and a number of derivations. Such designs represent a dramatic break away from traditional ones; some would say a dramatic breakthrough, too. Outlines are generally well defined, conforming purely to artistic rather than to mathematical considerations. These might be a cluster of vivid orange lilies resting at the base of two slender and contorted twigs in a round stone pot, or a pair of vibrant golden gerberas among a tangle of burnt gorse branches; a trio of spherical allium heads linked by swirls of pampas leaves, or a simple vertical composition of iris leaves and a couple of anemones in a plain, cylindrical vase. When material is used with such clarity of line, the symbolism becomes apparent: a curving branch represents the calligraphic art, a robust piece of driftwood suggests strength and power, flowers suggest delicacy, and curving twigs contribute movement.

When flowers are used *en masse*, it is usually to achieve a dense colour concentration, and may be done in such a way that, visually, they lose their identity as plants. Other plant materials take on a new identity, and often greater visual appeal, as they are transformed with paint, bleach, or dye.

THE BACKGROUND STORY

Much of the perceived symbolism and grace of a flower arrangement depends on the background against which it is seen. Just as paintings in an art gallery are displayed on plain or rough-textured, single-colour walls, so a floral display is seen to best advantage against a background to which it is sympathetic, and in a position where there is adequate space around it. Even the Victorians, who loved

to clutter their rooms with ornaments and plants, understood this. Mrs Beeton, writing in her book of home management about the growing popularity of flower arrangements in the home, counselled her readers that 'care should be taken not to overload the table with flowers'; advice which, in a more general sense, is as timely today as it was a hundred years ago.

Naturally, the proposed background of a flower arrangement does not need to be plain; a patterned wallcovering or fabric or even a painting used to frame a floral display can be used to positive advantage. It is important to take into account the special features of a position, whether it is a stone fireplace in the sitting room, a Regency-striped niche in the dining room, a ladder unit in the hall, or a deep window seat in the bedroom. Each will have its own individual characteristics in terms of colour, pattern, texture, height, width, and space, and these will help to decide the shape, proportion, and colour composition of an arrangement. It

The cool, clear colours of the countryside in spring are blended together in a natural-looking way. The delicate white heads of sheep's parsley, or Queen Anne's lace, form a misty background for the sharp green spurge (euphorbia) and the curving stems of buttercup. The container is a stone mustard jar. **Opposite**

Petunias, largely overlooked in floral art, are arranged with chrysanthemums and clusters of feverfew in a red, blue, and white lustre jug. The sinuous lines of the arrangement follow those of the hand-painted design on the Chinese wall painting. **Left**

is an unwise arranger indeed, who exerts time and trouble creating a fulsome display of pink and yellow lilies, roses, and carnations, and then wanders from room to room trying to find a home for it!

The colour of a background can, in visual terms, make or break a flower arrangement, and can cause a design to pass almost unnoticed or be projected in the most flattering way. An intricately patterned background calls for special care in the choice of both container and plant materials: wallpaper that has a *trompe-l'oeil* effect of foliage or a vision of a leafy arbour could inspire floral arrangements that both harmonize with the background and are eye-catching in their own right. You could fill a tall glass jug with leaves on a starkly contrasting scale, with five hosta (plantain lily) or acanthus leaves and, for a colour highlight, a stem of orange crown imperial lilies. Or select a plain, bright vase, either red, orange, or yellow, and arrange it with curving branches of chestnut or lime. You could take a leaf-green container and arrange it with showy flowers like glossy red tulips or scarlet field poppies, or cover a cylindrical or rectangular vase, however modest, with a piece of the relevant wallpaper and, having achieved the ultimate in container harmony, arrange it with a bunch of complementary flowers such as sunset-pink peonies.

If the background illusion is floral rather than leafy, you can select the single most contrasting colour – yellow if the flowers are in the violet range – and concentrate on that. A yellow container, maybe a bright enamel fruit bowl, filled with predominantly yellow flowers in varying shapes and textures would be set off beautifully by the violet background.

In some cases, you can use a picture as a colour or design cue to a flower arrangement, or even as a background. An oil painting of a flowery meadow, an evocative composition of lush green grass speckled with campion, daisies, and buttercups, can prompt a design composed of similar flowers or others echoing the same colours. A green glass bowl arranged with a mound of country flowers could become a three-dimensional extension of the painting and, together, they would create an interesting still-life group.

In another vein, a painting or print can provide inspiration for an arrangement with strong visual associations to be placed in close proximity to it. A picture of an interior can stimulate ideas for an arrangement that would complement that setting. Place marigolds near a painting of a Provençal kitchen, for example. A harvest scene could be enhanced by a nearby basket of wheat and cornflowers, and a botanical study – a Redouté rose print, say – could be complemented by its real-life counterpart, a fragrant bowl of a similar variety of roses.

Whether the background is plain or patterned, light-coloured or dark, it is important to achieve a sense of proportion in any flower arrangement that is destined to be seen against it. A small beaker of primroses seen in isolation in front of an uninterrupted expanse of wall would have about as much impact as a miniature painting which was the sole exhibit in a spacious picture gallery. Move the spring posy to stand on a small table, which then becomes its background, or to form part of a group with other items – a collection of pillboxes or scent bottles, say – and it at once relates to them in scale and grows in visual importance.

As autumn approaches the floral colours echo those of the falling leaves and combine in a brilliant display of reds and golds. The preserve jars, a considered accessory, add visual weight at table level and balance the relative proportions of the container and plant materials. **Below left**

A basket of colourful garden flowers – a few pansies from one border, a handful of marigolds from another – makes a charming informal table decoration, equally suitable for an indoor or outdoor occasion. The matching basket of nectarines adds a look of luxury. **Opposite**

Large arrangements are not necessarily the best choice when faced with a large blank wall. Except on the most formal occasions, when either an urn filled to overflowing in the style of Dutch Old Masters, or a shapely pedestal design would take their rightful place in splendid isolation, it is a good idea to compose a still-life study with one or more flower arrangements taking prominence. You could gather together three pastel-coloured jugs in an Art Nouveau style, fill two of them with handfuls of country flowers such as roses and campanula (bellflowers) and the third with mixed foliage; or, on a more rustic note, arrange a collection of rough stone jars where they will be dramatically silhouetted against the wall, and place a trio of tall, stately amaryllis flowers in one of them.

When, on the other hand, an arrangement is destined to occupy a confined space such as a niche or an alcove, it is important to design it so it has, visually speaking, room to breathe. To return briefly to mathematical principles, a formal or stylized arrangement in such a situation looks best when it occupies about two-thirds of the height – say, the distance between a table or cupboard top and the top of the arch. It is no coincidence that that employs the 1½:1 proportion again, comprising two-thirds arrangement and one-third space.

ACCESSORIES AFTER THE FACT

Ornaments and natural materials ranging from shells and rocks to sculpture and other *objets* can enhance a flower arrangement by highlighting a colour, emphasizing the

texture of the container, suggesting a theme, or altering the proportion of a design. When, for example, a group of decorative preserve jars is placed next to an autumnal display of golden fruit and berries, the jars, filled perhaps with quince jelly, add visual weight to the base of the design, and form a link with the container and the subject of the arrangement.

You may have a jug which has an especially attractive texture, a pattern of raised dots, for example, which would be echoed by the placement of two or three, or even more, knobbly and textured gourds; or a Middle Eastern earthenware pot – a natural for a grouping of bleached and dyed plant materials – which suggests a surrounding group of similar earthy containers to create a significant still-life group.

You may compose a pretty, dome-shaped arrangement or an inverted curve in a delicate glass bowl, and place it beside an alabaster figurine such as a classic cupid. In that case the accessory, so much taller and more slender than the arrangement, changes the proportion of the design, which takes on an L-shape. The two units could be linked by tall tendrils of sweet peas extending beyond the

arrangement outline to follow the line of the figurine. You may, in quite a different mood, create an arrangement of silver-grey and pale blue statice, sea holly, and thistles to achieve a design that would be reminiscent of a foam-topped wave. To accentuate the symbolism and create a theme setting, you could surround the design with a pile of sea shells or a clutch of sea-washed pebbles, and add a thick knot of wispy rope or a piece of driftwood as a final inspired touch.

Perhaps the most widely used accessory of all is fruit. This was a favourite choice of both 17th-century and Victorian flower painters, possibly because it is so versatile. You can place a few lightly polished rosy apples beside a predominantly red flower arrangement to emphasize and reinforce the colour impact, to add gleaming highlights – especially effective when the principal flowers have a matt texture – and to add full, round shapes, an important 'extra' when a design is mainly composed of slender and arching materials.

You can use high-profile, mid-summer fruits to transform a design from a delightful arrangement into a delicious composition. A bowl of rich cherries enhances a casual display of sweet peas arranged in bunches, and creates an appetizing island of fruit and flowers on an expanse of green lawn. An earthenware bowl of just-ripe strawberries placed beside a pot of pastel-pale Shirley poppies emphasizes the graceful and ethereal quality of the flowers, and a slice of ruby-red watermelon beside a glass bowl of open roses contributes both high gloss and new textural dimension.

Citrus fruits can make powerful accessories, since they have a colour sharpness found in few flowers. Place a black woven basket of white marguerites or acrocliniums in a room furnished in monotones, place a lemon, an orange, or a lime beside it, and both the arrangement and the room will come alight. Arrange a trio of yellow lilies as the focal point in a low-colour arrangement, then echo and magnify their brightness with a lemon or two beside the container. Or use the fruits themselves as the focal point of an arrangement, threading them with stub wires and hooking them onto the holding material in place of full, round flowers.

TOOLS OF THE TRADE

A red enamel teapot holding aloft a display of scarlet tulips and delicate cream narcissus; an earthenware pot filled with a nosegay of roses and marigolds; a colourful jug brimming over with a handful of daisy chrysanthemums and vibrant geraniums – it is possible, and can be infinitely rewarding, to arrange jugs and vases of flowers and foliage without the use of any special holding material. Choose a container narrow enough to hold the stems

An appetizing arrangement for a summer lunch or supper party. The vineyard-style basket holds a harvest of strawberries speared on cocktail sticks, blended with spray chrysanthemums, sweet peas, and love-in-a-mist. It is advisable to have a reserve supply of fruit in case guests find the decoration irresistible. **Opposite**

A blackened griddle iron with its tall hoop handle makes a dramatic outline for a composition of fruit and flowers. The framework of lilies, laurel leaves, spindle berries, and seedheads is arranged first, then the wired fruits and nuts are pressed into the soaked foam to form a pyramid. **Right**

upright or just wide enough to allow them to fan out in the way you envisage, and you will not need recourse to the materials unromantically termed 'mechanics'.

As your interest in floral art develops and you want to compose arrangements with specific shapes, place stems at wayward angles, and adapt containers to all kinds of floral use, you will find a selection of water-holding and stem-holding materials especially useful. You will also want to build up your tool kit of other specialized equipment, which will make the task of preparing containers and harvesting and preparing plant materials both quicker and easier.

STEM-HOLDING MATERIALS

There are three principal means of holding stems in place in arrangements of fresh flowers and foliage: the use of crumpled wire netting, absorbent polystyrene foam, and metal pinholders. Other methods, such as pushing stems into a handful of pebbles in a decorative glass vase, have a more limited application.

The first of these materials, wire netting, is used to tame stems arranged in wide-necked containers such as large jugs or bowls and baskets fitted with an inner water-holding liner. You can buy plastic-covered netting with a 2.5cm (1in) mesh, of the kind shown in many of

Useful tools from left to right: Selection of pinholders, florists' scissors, absorbent stem-holding foam, sharp knives, florists' adhesive clay, narrow florists' adhesive tape, scissors, secateurs (pruning shears), plastic saucer, candle cup, and wire mesh netting. **Above**

FIXING FLORISTS' WIRE MESH NETTING

You Will Need

container with a large aperture • piece of plastic-covered florists' wire mesh netting • wire cutters • narrow florists' adhesive tape • scissors

Preparing a container in this way will help you to anchor stems of fresh or dried flowers in a casual and informal design.

Crumple the wire netting into a ball and place it in the neck of the container. If you wish to position some of the stems to slant at a low angle, ease the wire so that it forms a mound extending slightly above the level of the container rim. Remember that the lowest of the plant materials will have to be positioned so that they conceal this holding material.

Cut two lengths of tape slightly longer than the diameter of the container opening. Thread the first strip under the wire in two places, take it across the container, and stick it to the rim on each side. Cross the second strip at right angles to the first and fix it in the same way. Threading the tape under the wire ensures that the ball of wire does not slip down into the container.

As informal as can be – a collection of earthenware flowerpots topped by greeny-blue hydrangea heads could decorate the table for an outdoor buffet or barbecue, or a supper party in a farmhouse-style kitchen. **Left**

Cut out for a conservatory – this open-work vase is fitted with a plastic saucer of soaked foam to support a colourful cascade of godetia and sweet peas. **Opposite**

the project photographs, or use the type sold in garden centres for outdoor use. A piece of netting measuring about 24cm × 34cm (9in × 13in) is enough for most average-size containers, with proportionately smaller or larger pieces for other container types.

Crush the netting lightly in your hands to form it into a ball and push it into the neck of the container. If you are using uncovered netting, which will have a tangle of rough edges, in a precious container such as one made of silver or glass, take the precaution of first lining the inner rim with a protective layer of insulating tape.

Although the ball of wire should fit tightly into the container opening, it is advisable to secure it, to prevent it slipping or becoming lop-sided as you position the stems. To do this, use narrow florists' adhesive tape, which is sold in several colours – green, white, and brown

among them. When the lower flowers and leaves in a design will dip and trail low over the container rim and conceal the fixings, you can criss-cross two lengths of holding tape over the wire and down about 2cm (¾in) over the rim. When the rim will not be covered with plant materials in this way, and the tape might show, cut several short lengths, wrap each one around a piece of wire, and twist it inwards, to stick to the inside of the container. When you dismantle an arrangement, you can straighten out the wire and store it for future use.

The use of crumpled wire netting makes it possible to arrange, for example, three stems of Madonna lilies in a wide-necked vase, each stem facing in the direction you have determined. However, when you want the outline to be more adventurous, or more deliberately wayward, or if you want to position some stems horizontally or at a steep

downward angle, your choice of stem-holding material will be absorbent polystyrene foam. This material, which is sold under several brand names and is usually dull green, has had the most far-reaching and significant effect on the art of flower arranging, and has made possible shapes and outlines that could not otherwise have been achieved. The foam is sold in two main sizes: in 6cm (2½in) deep cylinders with an 8cm (3in) diameter, and in blocks measuring 22.5cm × 11cm × 7.5cm (9in × 4¼in × 3in), which you can cut to any size and shape.

Florists sell inexpensive plastic saucers, usually green or white, which have an indent just the right size to hold one of the foam cylinders, and plastic 'candle cups', made

with a cork-shaped plug that fits into the top of a candlestick. In this way, with a cylinder of stem-holding foam secured in a water-holding dish, you can convert a tall container or a household item, be it a wine carafe, decorative tin, or slender vase, into an improvised pedestal, and arrange arching stems to cascade attractively, dipping far below the rim.

The taller the converted container, the more precarious the foam holder may be. To attach a plastic saucer to the top of a tall vase, and hold the soaked foam securely in place, use a strip of florists' adhesive clay. This is another product sold under many trade names and which may be either brown or green. Press the clay around the rim of the

FIXING A SAUCER OF STEM-HOLDING FOAM

By preparing a container in this way you can use a tall vase, carafe, or jug as a pedestal, positioning flower and foliage stems to slant both downwards and horizontally.

1 Cut small lengths of adhesive clay and press them onto the underside of the plastic saucer, where it will come into contact with the top of the container. Press the saucer firmly in place to hold it securely.

You Will Need

tall container ● strip of florists' adhesive clay ● plastic foam-holding saucer, or you could use an upturned coffee jar lid ● cylinder of stem-holding foam, absorbent or dry according to the materials to be arranged ● narrow florists' adhesive tape ● scissors

A highly-polished brass candlestick becomes a pedestal container when it is fitted with a plastic saucer and a cylinder of soaked foam. The dome of cypress and ivy leaves forms a foundation for a casual placement of freesias and tulips. **Right**

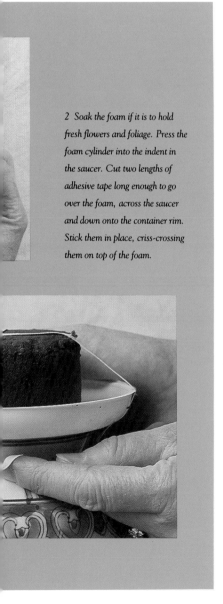

2 Soak the foam if it is to hold fresh flowers and foliage. Press the foam cylinder into the indent in the saucer. Cut two lengths of adhesive tape long enough to go over the foam, across the saucer and down onto the container rim. Stick them in place, criss-crossing them on top of the foam.

container or saucer, and press the saucer firmly in place. Insert the cylinder of soaked foam and criss-cross two strips of narrow florists' adhesive tape over it, down over the rim of the saucer and, for extra security, onto the container. If the flower arrangement thus elevated is to be composed of heavy materials, such as substantial stems of foliage or shrubs, it is advisable to weight the container first with ballast. A glass container will need presentable materials such as glass marbles, coloured pebbles, or coloured sand; others can be held steady with a few handfuls of sand, soil, or gravel.

Absorbent foam blocks have many applications in flower arrangements, ranging from massive to miniature. You may need to use a block standing on end for a tall arrangement in a deep basket, or two blocks side-by-side for a larger design. Cut strips to fit inside square or rectangular containers or to wedge in the neck of other shapes, or use a cube of the material in a dish to create an L-shaped design in light or middleweight materials.

Cut the foam when it is dry, and keep the off-cuts, however small, to use at other times. You may, for example, want to pack a wide container with crushed and soaked foam, a method of anchoring stems that may be used when a mound of crumpled wire netting or a protruding block of foam could not be concealed by the plant materials. Whenever you want to position stems to slant downwards or lie horizontally, cut the foam so it extends about 2.5cm (1in) above the rim of the container;

it is this extra height that allows them to do so. Shape the foam so that there will be enough space around it to top up the container with water and keep the material permanently moist.

Soak the foam in a bowl of cold water until it has absorbed its capacity – this will take about 20 minutes. Once it is in place in an arrangement, top it up with water every day and, when the design is dismantled, store the foam in a plastic bag or box until you want to use it again. If you allow it to dry out, it will not reabsorb moisture.

The third principal means of anchoring stems is by using a pinholder, a flat heavy weight sold in a range of sizes and a variety of shapes, and which has a series of vertical pins arranged close together in straight rows. A pinholder may be used in the base of a deep container to anchor long or especially heavy stems, whether or not crumpled netting is used at the neck; and in flat dishes when, for example, an L-shaped design is created. Stems may in this case be pushed both vertically and horizontally between the spikes and the stem ends covered with water. Fix the pinholders to the base of a dry container with a few dabs of florists' adhesive clay, and conceal them, in shallow containers, with granite chippings, small pebbles or broken glass.

TOOL KIT

Beyond the stem-holding materials and the means of fixing them, there are a few items that are useful in the care and preparation of plant materials.

- A good-quality pair of secateurs or pruning shears are a 'must' for cutting branches and other woody stems. Dry the secateurs after use, and keep them in a dry place.
- Florists' scissors are useful for cutting less substantial flower and foliage stems, both in the garden and at the work table.
- A craft knife with a short, sharp blade is useful for scraping the bark from woody stems and splitting the stem ends, both ways of enabling the plant material to take up moisture.
- A watering-can with a thin spout is useful for topping up containers with water and is more efficient than a jug, which may cause spills and surface damage.
- A water spray or plant mister that emits a fine, even mist is invaluable for spraying fresh flower arrangements before you place them in position, and for giving them frequent cooling-down showers, especially in hot weather. Remember to remove arrangements to a water-resistant surface before spraying them.

In summer a large, open fireplace becomes a stage for an ever-changing floral display. The willow basket, lined with a deep bowl and two blocks of soaked foam, holds a countrified arrangement of wild flowers – daisy-like marguerites, campion, and buttercups. **Opposite**

A bright spot of colour anywhere you may need it in the garden, on the patio or balcony – a wooden garden basket arranged with a towering asymmetrical display of cereals, grasses, dahlias, and chrysanthemums in vibrant and harmonizing colours. **Below**

HARVESTING AND SELECTING FLOWERS

No matter how casual or carefully calculated an arrangement may be, no matter what, if any, holding material is used, one consideration is paramount: all the plant material in the display, every flower and leaf, seedhead and berry must be in perfect condition. This means you must harvest materials from the garden or countryside when they are in the peak of condition, and be critically selective whenever you purchase flowers from a florist or market stall.

In general, it is best to leave flowers to reach a mid-way stage of maturity on the plant. Cut rosebuds and carnations as they are just beginning to unfurl, and when tall spires – including larkspur, delphinium, gladioli, Canterbury bells, and orchids – are showing the full beauty of only the lower florets. Other florets will be at various stages of development all the way up the stem to the tightly-closed top-most buds, which are suitable candidates for use as 'points' in geometric designs. At this stage, plant materials are advanced enough to survive without further nutrition from the plant, and will give you the joy of watching them unfold day by day. Of course, there will be times when you will want to gather a handful of fully-opened roses with each delicate petal spread out, or a bunch of papery poppies to put on the kitchen table. Theirs will be a short vase-life, but a beautiful one.

It is important to plan your harvesting time with something of the precision of a farmer garnering his crops. Avoid cutting flowers and foliage in the heat of the sun, when they are at their most vulnerable and least able to recover from the transition from growing plant to design component. In any case, especially in hot weather, it is best to put stems straight into water as soon as they are cut. For large stems – an armful of dahlias or branches of privet – this may mean taking a bucket of cool water from patch to patch. For smaller materials – a handful of marigolds or a few stems of freesia – you can simply carry a bowl of water in the basket over your arm.

Whether they are the fruits of your own harvest or a selective purchase, treat flower and foliage stems carefully as soon as you bring them indoors, using a simple process known as 'conditioning'. Strip off any leaves that would come below the water line, since these would sour the water and shorten the vase-life of the material. Using sharp secateurs (pruning shears) or florists' scissors, recut the stem ends at a sharp angle, to allow the largest possible area to soak up moisture. In the case of hollow and fleshy stems such as daffodil and delphinium, do this

under water, the stems held just below the water line in a bowl. This extra precaution helps prevent the formation of air locks, which inhibit moisture intake and, again, shorten the vase-life of the flowers.

Stand all the stems in cool – not ice-cold – water for at least a couple of hours, longer if possible. Wrap bunches of flowers such as tulips and ranunculus, which have a bad reputation for drooping, in newspaper, and stand them up to their necks – but not over the flower heads – in water.

Once the plant material has had a long, reviving drink, take a critical look at each stem. Snip off damaged leaves, and remove all the leaves from flowers such as spray chrysanthemums, which do not have the staying

Completely at home in its surroundings, the small pottery basket is arranged with buttercups and daisies and a single marguerite – a daisy look-alike on a larger scale. The design would also look at home in a young child's room. **Opposite**

Tulips can have a wayward look. Use this to advantage by positioning the stems to curve in different directions, while composing a well-ordered cluster of leaves and flowers at the heart of the design. **Above**

power of the blooms. Examine each flower carefully, and gently pick off any damaged outer petals – those of roses, for instance – which spoil the beauty of an otherwise perfect specimen.

Heat and light are significant factors in the development and longevity of the cut stems, just as they are when plants are growing. If you want to hold back the development of cut flowers – say, for a party two or three days ahead – keep them in water in a cool, dark place or even, where small quantities are concerned, in the refrigerator. If, on the other hand, you are impatient for flowers to open more readily stand them in warm water, in a warm place for a few hours.

The twin elements, heat and light, have equally significant effects on the lasting qualities of a completed arrangement. It is important to spray fresh flowers with a fine mist of cool water at least once a day and more frequently in hot weather, and to shelter them from direct heat or sunlight. No matter how tempting it may be to place an arrangement of fresh or dried flowers where it will be lit by the full force of the summer sun, don't do it; or, at least, not for long. Position it in a sheltered spot, beside the window but not facing it, or on a table, desk, chair or stool – anything but a shelf over a radiator.

Gradually the flowers will fade. Postpone this process for as long as possible by removing them from the container and recutting the stem ends, and giving them fresh water every day. Discard some short-lived species, and replace them with others; a fresh bunch of paper-white narcissus set among a bevy of lilies, tulips, and spray carnations will help to rejuvenate the arrangement's decorative potential.

ROMANTIC INTERLUDE

You Will Need

wide-necked jug • piece of plastic-covered wire mesh netting • narrow florists' adhesive tape • scissors • flowers such as roses, carnations, freesias, lilies • light-textured foliage such as ming or maidenhair fern • florists' scissors

A beautiful old hand-painted jug, surely a family heirloom, was the keynote of this uncompromisingly romantic bedside group. The subtle scents of summer's prettiest blooms – roses, carnations, and freesias – mingle to become a fresh-flower potpourri.

1 Pale pink and partly-opened roses, which form a more attractive composition than tightly-furled buds, form the heart of the design and echo the pattern on the container. Glossy highlights are provided by the shiny petals of the sharp yellow lilies and the trumpet-shaped freesias. The short foliage sprays, which will be arranged in a ring around the rim of the jug, give the flower group a natural, straight-from-the-garden look.

2 Crumple the wire mesh netting into a ball and fit it into the neck of the jug, so that it forms a mound extending above the rim. Criss-cross two pieces of adhesive tape, threading them through the netting and sticking the ends to the container. Check the netting is held firmly in place. Position a tall stem of foliage at the back of the container, and a ring of roses through the centre.

3 Continue the group by positioning more roses, their stems cut to varying lengths so that the flowers are graduated in height. Begin positioning the lilies between the roses, the large star-shaped flowers contrasting with the full, compact ones.

4 Add more lilies, at varying heights throughout the arrangement, then the carnations and the freesias, cutting some stems short so that the flowers rest close to the rim of the container.

5 Add the soft, feathery foliage throughout the design, so that it separates some of the flowers and allows them to be seen in clear outline. Arrange some short stems of foliage around the rim of the jug, where it will conceal the mound of wire mesh netting.

ORIENT EXPRESS

You Will Need

tall Oriental-style vase ● piece of plastic-covered wire mesh netting ● narrow florists' adhesive tape ● scissors ● flowers such as lilies, delphinium, and spider chrysanthemums ● foliage such as ming and pampas ● florists' scissors

An elegant blue and white patterned vase suggests a composition in the traditional Oriental flower colours of yellow, white and blue. Simplicity is the key. The three flower types are complemented with delicate sprays of ming foliage.

1 Choose flowers in clear, crisp colours and in shapes that contrast sharply with each other. Designs inspired by those of the Orient should have clear, uncluttered lines and the plant material should be well-defined.

2 Crumple the wire mesh netting into a ball and shape and press it into the neck of the container. Thread two strips of florists' adhesive tape through the wires and cross them over the mound and onto the container rim. Cut the stems of the lilies in varying lengths, so that the flower heads will range in height.

3 Position the stems of the spider chrysanthemums so that the flower clusters form a ring around the lilies, concealing some of their stems.

4 Add the blue accents, the delphinium flowers that echo the colour of the vase decoration. These flowers nestle against the lily stems, partially concealing them.

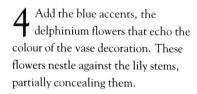

5 Arrange the stems of ming foliage around the rim of the vase. Position a few stems of pampas grass foliage at one side of the arrangement, to cascade over the vase.

THE WILD LOOK

You Will Need

tall, wide basket • waterproof liner such as a plastic bowl • block of absorbent stem-holding foam, soaked in water • narrow florists' adhesive tape • scissors • selection of materials such as drying oak leaves, dried arbutus leaves, dried poppy seedheads, teasels, wheat, old man's beard, rosehips, rose 'mossballs' • secateurs (pruning shears) • clear varnish (optional)

As winter approaches it is both exhilarating and rewarding to set off in search of countryside treasures. You may find oak leaves turning from green to yellow, vibrant rosehips and haws, a few stray stalks of wheat, dried poppy seedheads and teasels, and fluffy tufts of old man's beard (*Clematis vitalba*) – enough to compose a basket to set in the garden room or anywhere that will catch shafts of autumn sunlight.

1 A craftsman's basket was chosen for this design – one traditionally used by Greek olive pickers. Its close, even weave and almost smooth texture lends itself to the overall effect. A more rustic and rugged container might overshadow the neutral tones and subtle textures of the wayside materials. Gather as many of the rosehips as you can, the brighter the better.

2 Place the plastic bowl or other liner in the basket and put the block of soaked foam in place. It can be secured in position by taking adhesive tape from side to side and front to back, over the foam and down on the basket rim. Position the first stems of oak, the tallest one off-centre at the back and another, well curved and twisted, low over the front on the same side. Position a short stem of oak leaves at the front on the opposite side.

3 Add the tall stem of contrasting leaves, in this case dried and sun-bleached arbutus. Then arrange a cluster of wheat stalks. The ones chosen here curved naturally to one side, arching over the basket rim and giving the impression of a field of wheat swaying in the breeze.

4 The textural contrast builds up. Add teasels of varying lengths, the furry 'mossballs' from a wild rose bush, and the dried poppy seedheads. Cut some stems short so that the plant material rests against the basket rim.

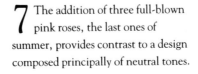

5 Position the rosehips in clusters as dense as your supply will allow. The arrangement benefits from a generous profusion of the rich, glossy red colour. If you wish, paint or spray the berries with clear varnish.

6 Complete this wild-looking and asymmetrical design by adding short sprays of fluffy old man's beard where they will contrast strikingly with the solid shapes of the poppy seedheads and the high gloss of the rosehips.

7 The addition of three full-blown pink roses, the last ones of summer, provides contrast to a design composed principally of neutral tones.

SHEER ELEGANCE

You Will Need

tall, shapely jug • piece of plastic-covered wire mesh netting • narrow florists' adhesive tape • scissors • selection of flowers such as Euphorbia fulgens, *larkspur, and roses • foliage such as eucalyptus • florists' scissors*

A container with classic lines suggests a stylish but uncluttered composition that in no way detracts from the distinctive pattern. The use of a foam-holding saucer and a cylinder of soaked foam enables the stems to be angled in a curve that echoes the lines of the jug.

1 The flowers are chosen to emphasize and complement the colours of the Gothic-style pattern on the jug. The *Euphorbia fulgens* is a bright interpretation of the rust-red arches, the blue of the larkspur a lighter version of the background colour, and the roses a slightly richer shade of the cream of the figures.

3 Begin adding the blue flowers, to provide rich contrast with the euphorbia. Tall, stately stems of delphinium or larkspur occupy the centre ground of the design and form a dense background for the delicate cream roses.

2 Crumple the wire mesh netting into a ball and fit it into the neck of the container. Ease the wire upwards so that it forms a mound extending above the neck of the jug. Thread two strips of adhesive tape through the wire, criss-cross it over the mound and stick the ends onto the container. Arrange arching stems of the euphorbia, cut to varying lengths, so that the vibrant flowers and leaves cascade over one side of the jug.

4 Cut the rose stems to varying lengths and split or cut the stem ends so that the flowers will have the best chance of a long vase-life. Position the stems so that the flowers form a fan shape at the front of the arrangement.

5 Complete the arrangement by positioning some foliage stems to arch over the handle of the jug and balance the cascade of euphorbia. This will prevent a lop-sided look. Cut off any euphorbia leaves that look particularly wayward and may spoil the overall shape of the design.

THE MODERN APPROACH

You Will Need

*tall, wide cylindrical vase ● piece
of plastic-covered wire mesh netting
● narrow florists' adhesive tape
● scissors ● selection of flowers
such as white lilies, and cream and
white roses ● contrasting foliage
types such as acanthus, eucalyptus,
and pampas grass ● florists' scissors*

A tall, wide cylindrical vase spatter-painted to harmonize with the wall behind it is on just the right lines for a low-key floral display in a modern setting. The flowers and foliage stems are arranged so that the materials form a dense, closely-integrated pattern, light materials against dark ones, stately lilies contrasting with delicate roses.

1 The most striking feature of this design is not the lilies, but the large, deep green and glossy acanthus leaves which allow all the flowers to be seen in sharp outline. You could substitute fig, *Fatsia japonica* or hosta (plantain lily) leaves, among others, to create a similar effect. In place of the pampas grass leaves you could use slender stems of broom.

3 Position the lily stems so that the fully-opened flowers are pointing in different directions – some forward, some to the right, and some to the left. In this way you can appreciate the full beauty of these flowers in silhouette.

2 Crumple the wire mesh netting into a ball and fit it into the neck of the container. Thread two lengths of adhesive tape through the netting, criss-cross them over the container and stick the ends close to the rim, where they will be concealed by the lowest of the plant materials. Arrange the acanthus stems so that the leaves form a bowl shape to outline the flowers, with the tallest stems at the back and the lowest ones at the front.

4 Cut off all but the top-most rose leaves, to prevent a crowded mass in the heart of the design. Split the ends of the rose stems to facilitate water intake.

5 Arrange the roses so that they nestle among the lily stems and give an overall roundness to the design. Add short sprays of foliage, such as eucalyptus, to trail over the container rim, and a few strands of pampas foliage at one side.

COUNTRY STYLE

A medley of cottage-garden flowers vividly contrasting in shape, texture, and colour are arranged just as they might grow in a border – intermingled and in profusion. The jug, a junk shop find, was crackle-painted to match the wall.

1 To achieve this country look, choose flowers which contrast with each other in every way. These can vary according to season.

2 Crumple the wire mesh netting into a ball and fit it into the neck of the jug so that it forms a mound above the rim. Criss-cross two pieces of adhesive tape over the wire, threading them through it in several places and sticking the ends to the container. Arrange the arched stems of euphorbia so that they droop over the jug handle, on one side only.

3 Arrange the goldenrod stems so that they form a pyramid shape, with the tallest ones in the centre and progressively shorter ones at the front and sides.

4 Position the delphinium stems among the goldenrod and towards the back of the design. Some stems should be long enough for the contrasting blue flowers to be seen in detail against the yellow.

5 Arrange the round, flat-faced marigold flowers at varying heights so that they are seen in a circular formation. Select the best, brightest specimen to place in the centre front, where it will overlap the rim of the jug. In a more formal arrangement, this would be considered the focal point.

TRADITIONAL VALUES

A two-handled glass urn, the type of container popular in 18th-century compositions, holds a classic combination of flowers in pastel tints of pink, peach, and cream. The romantic roses contrast well with the trumpet shapes of the Peruvian lilies and freesias.

1 To achieve the near-symmetry of the arrangement, which is broken only by a couple of stems of freesia placed low over the rim, you need a balanced container, one with two handles, or no handles at all. An urn-shaped vase would be equally suitable. If possible, include some foliage which is variegated, so that it contributes to the lightness of the design.

2 Cut short lengths of adhesive clay and press onto the underside of the plastic saucer. Press the saucer onto the rim of the container. Position the cylinder of soaked foam in the saucer indent, and secure it in place by criss-crossing two strips of adhesive tape over the foam and the saucer and sticking the ends on the container. Arrange the various types of foliage to form the outline of the design, with some stems trailing low over the rim of the container on each side. Cut short sprays of the flowering shrub and arrange them between the sprays of variegated foliage, emphasizing the triangular shape of the outline.

3 Arrange long stems of a slender foliage type to give height to the design. If you wish the arrangement to conform to formal lines, the foliage tips should be confined to the triangular shape. Longer, more wayward-looking stems add a touch of informality.

4 Cut individual stems from some of the Peruvian lilies and position them at the heart of the design, close to the foam and among the sprays of flowering shrub. Arrange longer stems within the triangular outline.

5 Fill in the design with partly-opened roses, reserving the prize bloom for the centre front position, low over the container rim.

6 Arrange the freesias between the roses where their differing shapes and tints will form a flattering contrast. Arrange short stems of foliage such as eucalyptus at the heart of the design and, for a finishing touch, add a couple of stems of foliage and freesias slanting almost vertically to one side.

A BOLD STATEMENT

You Will Need

deep, wide, bowl-shaped container
* *piece of wire mesh netting*
* *narrow florists' adhesive tape*
* *scissors* ● *flowers such as*
mimosa, irises, carnations, and
anemones ● *florists' scissors*

The boldest statement you can make is to arrange flowers in the three primary colours – red, yellow, and blue – at full strength. This eye-catching arrangement is suitable for an entrance hall or a landing, or as the centre-piece of a buffet table where the party is in full swing.

1 If possible, choose a plain container in one of the flower colours, or one with a bold pattern in primary colours. A yellow enamel salad bowl was used here, to match the brilliance of the mimosa.

2 Crumple the wire mesh netting and fit it into the bowl. Cut short strips of adhesive tape, wrap one end around the wire close to the rim, and bring the tape over and along the vessel, just inside the rim. Repeat this around the bowl to secure the wire and check that it has no freedom of movement. Lightly crush the ends of the mimosa stems, scrape off about 5cm (2in) of the bark and split the ends with a sharp knife. Arrange the mimosa evenly around the container to create a dome shape.

3 Cut the iris stems to different lengths and arrange them so that the colour is evenly distributed throughout the design, and the height is graduated.

4 The design features five red
carnations. Arrange them to
create a pyramid effect with the colour
evenly balanced throughout the group.

5 Arrange a few red anemones close
to the rim of the container where,
against the yellow of the bowl, they will
provide the sharpest contrast of all.

COMPLETE HARMONY

You Will Need

thick, sturdy container such as a mustard jar or other earthenware pot ● florists' adhesive clay ● scissors ● plastic foam-holding saucer ● cylinder and small piece of absorbent stem-holding foam, soaked in water ● narrow florists' adhesive tape ● selection of plant materials such as lilies, irises, anemones, larkspur, flowering shrub, pyracantha (firethorn) berries, spiky evergreen leaves ● florists' scissors ● secateurs (pruning shears)

In this design, primary blue and secondary orange, colours which face each other on the colour wheel, demonstrate the attraction of opposites. The composition was inspired by the modern abstract painting in the background; it would look equally dramatic against a plain blue or orange wall and positively brilliant against green.

1 The arrangement is designed as an exuberant burst of colour, like rays of the sun radiating from the central point. The lilies and irises, which both form star-like shapes, contribute to this effect. The two mustard jars, one used as the container and the other as an accessory, have been painted with enamel, the paint drizzled and left to run in uneven lines.

2 Cut short lengths of the adhesive clay and press onto the underside of the plastic saucer. Press the saucer onto the top of the container. Put the soaked foam cylinder in place in the saucer indent and secure it with two criss-crossing strips of adhesive tape taken over the foam and saucer and stuck onto the top of the container. Arrange the foliage stems to make a fanburst shape, the tallest ones at the back and shorter ones on either side. Position the stems of pyracantha (firethorn) berries low on one side of the design. Cut short lengths of the flowering shrub and place close against the foam. Position the first of the blue flowers in a fan shape.

3 The dramatic colour is already apparent. Place the iris stems well apart so that the flowers will not appear crowded in the finished arrangement. Position the anemones, the only round, flat flower shapes, low at the front of the design.

4 Cut off some of the lily leaves, to avoid a confusion of foliage. Cut the stems in varying lengths so the flowers will be equally balanced throughout the arrangement. Add more foliage stems to create a visual dividing line between the flowers.

5 Cut two short stems of iris and push them into the small piece of soaked stem-holding foam. When the arrangement is in position in the room, place the second container beside it, and conceal the foam in its depths, so that the flowers appear to be spilling out of the jar.

RED ALERT

High drama is achieved by arranging flowers in a single hue, especially when the container – in this case a stylish biscuit (cookie) tin – strikes the same note. The addition of the white flowering shrub brings a touch of freshness to the design, and allows the full, rounded shape of the carnations to be seen in clear outline.

1 If possible, choose stems of the euphorbia, or a substitute flower, which have graceful curves, some to one side and some the other. The cascade effect this creates is important to the finished design. Three carnations are all you need to achieve a good visual balance, with sprays of their smaller counterparts, in a similar colour, serving as fillers.

2 Cut short strips of the adhesive clay and press onto the underside of the plastic saucer, where it will come into contact with the neck of the container. Press the saucer onto the top of the container and press the cylinder of soaked foam into the saucer indent. Secure the stem-holding material by criss-crossing two lengths of adhesive tape over the foam and the saucer and sticking them onto the top of the container. Cut the stems of eucalyptus to graduated lengths and position so that they arch in a small cascade on either side of the container. Arrange sprays of the flowering shrub to form a triangular outline above the container.

3 Cut the euphorbia stems in pairs of equal lengths and arrange on each side of the container to form a floral cascade, following the lines set by the eucalyptus. Cut off any wayward leaves that detract from the shape.

4 Arrange three carnations in a triangle, one at the top of the design, one slightly shorter on one side and one even shorter on the other. Begin filling in the gaps with stems of spray carnation.

5 Complete the arrangement by adding more spray carnations and stems of slender and pointed foliage. Be sure to place some stems so that the leaves trail down almost vertically, partially obscuring the tin. When a container has such a distinctive pattern as this one, with bold lettering, the flowers, even red ones, are in danger of being overshadowed by comparison.

6 When similar flowers are arranged in a jade green jug, the design becomes 'complementary' – a blend of two opposing colours on the colour wheel, each of which shows the other to best advantage. A composition like this, vibrant in its harmonious use of red and green, is particularly effective at Christmastime.

BLUE AND MAUVE

You Will Need

container such as a coffee pot, teapot, or jug ● florists' adhesive clay ● scissors ● plastic foam-holding saucer ● cylinder of soaked stem-holding foam ● narrow florists' adhesive tape ● foliage such as eucalyptus and flowering shrub ● secateurs (pruning shears) ● flowers such as irises, anemones, and freesias

This casual yet radiant arrangement spans the divisions between blue and mauve, two neighbouring colours on the colour wheel. The patterned coffee pot, in rich creamy yellow, is integrated into the design by the yellow flashes of the irises.

1 Grey-green foliage such as eucalyptus blends especially well with the mauve and blue floral scheme. Other good choices would be ballota and senecio, with purple sage used as a filling material.

2 Cut two strips of adhesive clay and press onto the base of the saucer. Press the saucer onto the top of the container. Position the foam in the saucer and secure it with two lengths of adhesive tape, taken over the foam and onto the container. The eucalyptus stems are arranged in a lop-sided triangular shape to create the design outline. Short sprays of flowering shrub are placed close to the foam .

3 Arrange the irises among the foliage, to follow the outline and reinforce the shape of the design.

4 Arrange the anemones between the irises, so that the deep purple and blue flowers alternate to create the colour harmony. Among the bunch of anemones is a two-tone flower, placed centrally, as the focal point.

5 Position the freesias to form a cascade effect on one side, the flowers dipping low over the handle of the pot and following the line of the foliage. Fill in any gaps with short sprays of foliage.

6 The same arrangement with daffodils in place of the anemones. When deep violet is replaced by brilliant yellow, the colour-wheel opposite of mauve, the design becomes 'complementary' or 'contrasting', taking on a new and vivid brightness. Sprays of mimosa reinforce the springtime brilliance.

A PERFECT COMPLEMENT

You Will Need

1 large melon ● knife ● dessert spoon ● plastic foam-holding saucer ● cylinder of absorbent stem-holding foam, soaked in water ● narrow florists' adhesive tape ● scissors ● selection of flowers such as mauve Singapore orchids, carnations, yellow mimosa, lilies, and roses ● foliage such as eucalyptus ● secateurs (pruning shears) ● florists' scissors

When mauve and yellow, two opposite colours on the colour wheel, are arranged together the result is sure to be both high-profile and eye-catching. Add to the impact of the design by using a scooped-out melon, with its deeply-ridged texture, as the unusual container.

1 Fruits and vegetables make interesting short-term containers; you can dry the shells in an oven at low temperature for a more permanent display. Watermelons, pumpkins and marrows (squash), or oranges and lemons can also be used.

Choose flowers which contrast dramatically with each other in both shape and texture – the huge, glossy yellow lilies and the tiny fluffy mimosa flowers are perfect examples.

2 Cut a thin slice from the top of the melon, and a sliver from the base so that it will stand steadily. With the spoon, scoop out the melon seeds into a bowl. Scoop out the melon flesh into a second bowl, taking care not to pierce and damage the shell.

3 Press the plastic saucer over the top of the melon and press the soaked foam into the indent. Criss-cross two lengths of adhesive tape over the foam and saucer and down onto the melon shell. Arrange stems of mimosa to make an irregular shape.

4 Arrange the orchids to make a triangular outline, the tallest one in the centre and two slightly shorter stems at the sides. Position the carnations to give weight to the design at the top and sides. Cut the lily stems and position them at the heart of the design, where the fully-opened flowers will be seen head on.

5 Add the cream roses, positioning some at the back so that they will be viewed through the more prominent flowers, and one low at the right. Complete the design with light sprays of foliage, placing some on the left of the arrangement to balance the rose. Keep the foam permanently moist, adding water at least once a day.

HOGARTH CURVE

You Will Need

tall, slender container such as a candlestick or figurine vase
● *florists' adhesive clay* ● *scissors*
● *small waterproof container for foam (a plastic foam-holding saucer may be too large for many designs)*
● *block of stem-holding foam, cut to shape and then soaked* ● *knife*
● *narrow florists' adhesive tape*
● *curved foliage stems such as broom to create the outline*
● *other foliage such as smilax, variegated scented geranium, and flowering shrub* ● *flowers such as carnations, spray carnations, and spray chrysanthemums* ● *florists' scissors*

The design is named after the 18th-century English painter William Hogarth, who called the flowing curves 'the line of beauty'. The stems creating the upper and lower curves should be placed so the outline appears as one rhythmic and unbroken line, sometimes known as a 'lazy S'. The design may be composed so that the curve flows from either the right or the left.

1 It is important to select or coax foliage or flower stems into matching curves to form the outline of the design. These broom stems were twisted into a circle, secured with rubber bands, and left overnight. More substantial stems may need to be soaked first, to make them supple.

2 Cut two short lengths of adhesive clay, press onto the underside of the foam holder and press the holder on top of the container. Position the foam in the container. Tape from side to side and front to back, over the foam and onto the candlestick. The outline of the design begins to take shape, with the clusters of broom stems placed exactly opposite each other on either side of the protruding cylinder of foam. The delicate scented geranium leaves reinforce the centre of the S-shape, leaving the tips slender and wispy.

3 Cut the carnation stems short and place one on either side and one low at the centre front of the design, where it will mask the container and holding material.

4 Position two more carnations, one to create a central dome effect and the other at the back of the design. Cut short stems of spray carnations and position them to fill in the gaps and provide a colour contrast. Add spray carnations to follow the outline of the foliage.

5 Position short sprays of a light foliage, such as smilax, between the principal flowers, with others trailing low at the front and back of the design to mask every trace of the mechanics.

GEOMETRY LESSON

You Will Need

shallow waterproof dish such as a baking or serving dish ● florists' adhesive clay ● scissors ● pinholder ● selection of flowers such as irises, daffodils, and anemones ● selection of slender foliage ● florists' scissors ● concealing material such as broken windscreen (windshield) glass, gravel, pebble chippings etc.

Whoever would have thought, when learning about right-angled triangles, that the knowledge would be put to use in a flower arrangement! This design, an interpretation of the classic L-shape, is composed on a stoneware dish which has, by contrast, gentle curves.

1 Select flowers that are well suited to a watery theme. Those with glossy or wax-like petals such as irises, lilies, and tulips seem to have a special affinity with designs in which 'open water' is a feature. Select sword-shaped foliage for the exaggerated point of the design; lily, tulip, and montbretia are among the many possibilities.

2 Make sure the inside of the container is absolutely dry. Cut three short lengths of florists' adhesive clay and press onto the bottom of the pinholder. Position this to one side of the container and press firmly in place.

3 Define the shape of the L with long, straight stems of foliage placed at right angles to one another. Note that the principal upright stem is a little way in from the edge of the pinholder. Give balance to the design by placing a shorter stem to the left of the principal stem with another angled to the right.

4 Position the irises, pressing the stems firmly onto the pinholder spikes, so that the flowers follow the shape outlined by the leaves.

5 Position the daffodils to fill in the gaps and complement the contrasting shape of the irises. Place a cluster of short-stemmed anemones close to the pinholder, where the flowers will be seen as deep shadows, and add a few foliage sprays. Spoon the concealing material – in this case broken windscreen (windshield) glass – around the pinholder until it is completely hidden. Glass has the advantage – over pebbles and granite, for example – of catching and reflecting the light in an attractive way.

6 This is a design which would be equally appropriate in both formal and informal surroundings. Here it is featured in a country setting, with a complementary bunch of raffia-tied irises displayed as a short-term and eye-catching accessory. You could also use a bunch of evergreens or dried flowers as a wall decoration.

GENTLE SLOPE

Composed on a spatter-painted wine carafe, the design forms a diagonal line, softened by the cluster of delicate and pretty flowers at the centre. A pair of such designs, raised on their pedestal-like containers above the table surface and composed as mirror images of each other, would be suitable decorations for a buffet or party table.

1 It is useful to have tall, narrow containers to compose angled and curved designs, and to decorate a party table when space is a consideration. This one, a discarded wine carafe, was painted white, left to dry and then splashed with coral pink, a colour which tones perfectly with the roses and carnations.

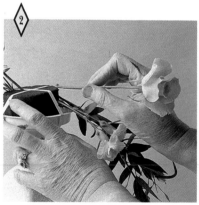

2 Cut strips of the adhesive clay and press onto the underside of the plastic saucer, where it will come into contact with the top of the container. Press the saucer in position, and place the soaked foam in the indent, securing it with two strips of adhesive tape criss-crossed over the foam and the saucer and stuck onto the container top. Define the line of the diagonal with two straight stems of foliage. Follow the outline with slender stems of spray carnations and strengthen it with the more rounded shapes of the roses.

3 Cut short sprays of goldenrod and place them slanting upwards on one side, and downwards on the other, to create a softened diagonal line. Cut one carnation stem very short and position it with the flower close against the foam.

4 Fill in the centre of the design with more carnations. Place short sprays of goldenrod to trail down over the rim of the container with others of a similar length making a gentle curve over the top. The effect is of an elongated oval.

5 Add short sprays of light foliage. To complete the design, cover the reverse. If it is to be viewed from all sides, arrange with a similar placement of flowers and leaves. If not, cover the foam and the plastic saucer with goldenrod, foliage, and just a few spray carnations.

ALL-ROUND SUCCESS

A design which is destined to be seen from all angles, as it would be in the centre of a dining table or occasional table, must be an all-round attraction. Turn the arrangement round one quarter of a circle as you compose it, and give it a final check to make sure it is worthy of every admiring glance.

1 We wanted a lush and luxurious look for this semi-formal centre-piece and chose a colour scheme in the rich, warm colours of velvet. A wide, bulbous pot was painted to give a feeling of 19th-century opulence. A brass, copper, or pewter pot, or any container in black, dark red, deep blue, purple, or forest green would be equally suitable.

2 Crumple the wire mesh netting into a ball and press it into the top of the container. Secure in place by threading two strips of florists' adhesive tape through the wire, criss-crossing them in the centre and sticking them to the top of the pot, where the ends will be concealed by the overhanging plant materials. Arrange the foliage to make a full shape all around the pot. Turn the container to check that the leaves are distributed evenly on all sides.

3 Work on one quarter of the arrangement at a time. Place short stems of euphorbia to arch over the side of the container at different levels. Position the anemones around the centre, alternating their colours to heighten the interest, and the spray carnations close to the container rim. Position the fully-opened roses at the heart of the design.

4 Compose the opposite side in a similar way, and fill in the gaps with short sprays of variegated foliage to separate the rich, deep colours of the flowers.

5 Turn the container around and repeat the design on the reverse, matching the first side in essence if not in detail. Polished wood makes a perfect surface for this rich-looking and jewel-bright arrangement.

INFORMAL TRIANGLE

A rectangular basket makes a perfect container for an informal arrangement on geometric lines – a triangular design in a country-style setting.

1 The arrangement is based on a classic triangular shape, with slender foliage stems and light weight sprays of goldenrod defining the points at the top and sides. For a more formal appearance, the basket could be replaced with a pottery or earthenware baking dish or a baking tin painted to suit the furnishings.

2 Place the liner in the basket, then the soaked foam. Hold the foam in place with two strips of florists' adhesive tape taken from front to back and side to side, stuck onto the container rim where it will be concealed by the plant materials. Position stems of foliage and sprays of goldenrod to define the outline of the design. To conform to the principles of a classic arrangement the height of the central stem should be at least 1½ times the longest measurement of the basket – in this case it is 35cm (13½in).

3 The cone-like shapes of the Peruvian lilies can be used to trace the pointed outlines of the design since they lead the eye naturally to the extremities. Cut the stems so that the flowers are positioned within those outlines, and cut off any leaves that would detract from the overall shape with their wayward curves. As always, cut the stems at a slanting angle, using sharp florists' scissors.

4 Position the carnations within the geometric outline, with two of the flowers placed close to the centre front of the design. Others should be positioned at the back of the arrangement, where they will be seen when the design is viewed from the sides. Fill in the gaps with spray chrysanthemums, with some individual flowers cut on short stems and placed close to the foam.

5 Complete the arrangement by filling in the gaps with goldenrod, the mass of tiny florets a softening influence on the more clearly defined outlines of the Peruvian lilies and roses.

STRAIGHT AND NARROW

An upright design verging on a classic vertical shape is ideal to display in a narrow alcove or niche; a pair of matching arrangements could enhance a sideboard or bookcase.

1 The quality and finish of the container you use is immaterial, since it is not seen in the finished design. Here a book will be used as a base, taking the place of a container to form a composite part of the arrangement. An old wooden or lacquered box could be used as a decorative stand in place of the book.

2 Place the soaked foam in the container. Outline the shape with the tallest, sword-shaped leaves of montbretia. It might be necessary to cut the ends to a point to make it easier to insert them into the foam. Arrange shorter stems of slender foliage to make a fan shape.

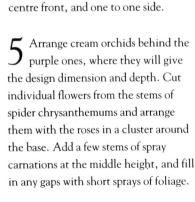

3 The deep purple orchids give the design a look of elegant luxury. Arrange them to follow the fan shape outlined by the green foliage. Position the stems so that the flowers are not touching each other; they should not look cramped or crowded.

4 Cut short the carnation stems and position two of the flowers in a straight line, one above the other at the centre front, and one to one side.

5 Arrange cream orchids behind the purple ones, where they will give the design dimension and depth. Cut individual flowers from the stems of spider chrysanthemums and arrange them with the roses in a cluster around the base. Add a few stems of spray carnations at the middle height, and fill in any gaps with short sprays of foliage.

FIRST AMONG UNEQUALS

An asymmetrical, or 'lop-sided' triangle is one of the classic geometric floral shapes. This arrangement, with deep coral pink two-tone carnations as the focal point, is well suited for display on a sideboard or side table.

1 A container with a slightly raised 'foot', facilitates an arrangement with side stems flowing downwards. You could equally well compose this design on a taller cake stand, or on a rectangular basket or wooden box in which the stem-holding foam extended about 5cm (2in) above the rim.

2 Cut two strips of adhesive clay and press onto the underside of the saucer. Press the saucer onto the stand, a little to the left of centre for a design that will flow to the right. Arrange the eucalyptus stems to etch in the height, with one tall, straight stem leaning slightly backwards and another, upright, in front of it. Position short stems flowing forwards on the left of the design with longer ones on the opposite side. Arrange the shorter stems of eucalyptus close to the centre, and others at the back of the design, to give balance and to cover the mechanics.

3 The freesias, with their narrow trumpet shapes, are used as 'points' in the design, following the outline of the triangle, with one in the centre to carry the colour through from the top to the bottom. The anemones, which are seen as small 'rounds', alternate with the freesias within the arrangement.

4 Position the three large 'rounds' – the carnations – to form the focal point, with one placed low and close to the rim of the container. Add more filler material – the flowering shrub – at the back of the design, where it will be seen through the foliage.

5 Complete the design with more short stems of flowering shrub and with forward-flowing stems of eucalyptus to break up the line of the container rim.

NAUTICAL THEME

You Will Need

*wooden box with a lid ● florists'
adhesive clay ● scissors ● small
waterproof container such as an
upturned coffee jar lid ● slice
cut from a cylinder of absorbent
stem-holding foam, soaked in water
● wooden cocktail sticks (if
needed) ● selection of flowers such
as irises, spray chrysanthemums,
and spray carnations ● foliage such
as eucalyptus ● florists' scissors*

A brass-lidded box opens to reveal a horizontal display with a nautical flavour. This design, with flowers in blue, bronze, and white, is suitable for a man's desk, and is narrow enough to be placed on a bookshelf.

1 The brass-lidded box gives character to the arrangement, though the glint of the metal cannot be seen from a straight-on view. You could use a sewing or needlework box, a child's pencil box, or a paintbox for a similar effect. You need a small waterproof holder for the foam slice – a purpose-made plastic saucer is too large for such a narrow arrangement.

2 Cut strips of adhesive clay and press to the underside of the foam holder, where it will come into contact with the divisions in the box. Press the foam holder firmly in place. Wedge the box open with the cocktail sticks if needed. Position stems of eucalyptus to make a long, low, trailing shape. The tallest central stem should define the outline of a low triangle.

3 Position the irises within the outline defined by the foliage. Some of the flowers should slant downwards and forwards on either side of the stem-holding foam.

4 Arrange the spray carnations around the irises, positioning the pencil-thin buds at the points of the design.

5 Fill in the gaps with the round, flat flowers. In this example, bronze spray chrysanthemums were used, their colour echoing the flash on the iris petals.

FLOWERS FOR SPECIAL OCCASIONS

~

You may have been asked to arrange the flowers for a church festival or a friend's wedding; you may want to give your home an extra sparkle for a party or at Christmastime, or compose a floral gift to mark an anniversary. Whatever the occasion, flowers make it all the more memorable, and arranging them becomes a special challenge.

The following pages take you through every stage of the planning, from measuring up the setting to estimating how many flowers you will need; from preparing a pedestal to composing an elegant bouquet for a bride. And, in keeping with centuries of tradition, we explore the many decorative roles of floral swags and garlands, circlets and wreaths.

Whatever the time of year, whatever the occasion, when there is a ring around the calendar and something to celebrate, flowers and foliage set the scene, whether a 'spring garden' arrangement of daffodils and tulips entwined around a branch in celebration of Easter; a shower of orchids and roses to be carried by a bride on her wedding day; a flamboyant pedestal arrangement of flowers spanning the colours of the rainbow, designed to be the focal point at a buffet party; an amusing composition of vivid flowers and cola cans for a children's tea party; or a sophisticated garland of evergreens to decorate the home at Christmastime.

Since the earliest times, and in civilizations and cultures all around the world, people have garlanded their homes and places of worship with flowers, hung wreaths of welcome or hoped-for good fortune on their doors, crowned their heroes with circlets of leaves, and presented nosegays of flowers to dignitaries and honoured guests. In pagan times, week-long festivals were held in celebration of the profusion of spring flowers, in anticipation of a plentiful harvest, and in acceptance of the onset of winter. With only primitive means of illumination, people brightened their homes in winter by bringing in glossy evergreens – which they believed to have magical powers not possessed by deciduous trees which had lost their leaves – to lighten their darkness.

Many of the floral traditions we carry on today have their origins and cultural roots in these prehistoric times. Others, such as the exchange of Valentine tokens and the gift of flowers on Mother's Day, have a slightly shorter history, but are no less meaningful for that. And then there are all the other family and community occasions when we want to share our pride or happiness, mark an anniversary, or create a certain ambience, when the occasion just wouldn't be complete without flowers.

You may have been asked to help with the flower decorations in church for a wedding or religious festival; you may have been entrusted to create the floral designs for a bride and her attendants on her wedding day; you might be planning an especially formal dinner party to flatter or impress a special guest; or you might have invited a number of friends and neighbours to an impromptu party, and want your home or garden to match the warmth of your welcome. Whatever the occasion, and regardless of the degree of formality or informality, many of the same guidelines to arranging flowers apply. Think of a pedestal to decorate a church as an arrangement of complementary flower shapes, textures, and colours chosen to harmonize with the background, and composed on a stand. Think of a wedding bouquet as a derivation of a simple posy, arranged in a free-fall or circular shape; of a centre-piece for the most formal of dinner parties as an opportunity to make a positive virtue of design simplicity.

A portable feast of flowers for an outdoor party has a look of extravagant luxury. It is composed of a handful of mixed blooms with stems held in soaked stem-holding foam.
Right

And as for an impromptu party, when time is of the essence, look upon it as a chance to put your sense of colour and style into reflex action in a matter of moments. The special-occasion projects in this book are designed to guide you through all these events and more, taking each one step-by-step from its planning stage to the moment when, with a sigh of satisfaction, you step back to appraise – and admire – your work.

A delightful gift to celebrate the birth or baptism of a baby. Snippings of lime-green lady's mantle and white gypsophila, which serve as filler material, provide an important variation of shape and scale. **Below**

GARLANDS AND SWAGS

The earliest known floral decorations were not arrangements as we understand them, but garlands and swags,

ribbons and ropes, which were draped over altars and doorways, twisted around pillars and posts, and looped over, across, and around important pieces of furniture. And then there were wreaths and rings, circlets and hoops of flowers and foliage, which were worn on the head or around the neck, hung on walls and doors, placed on banqueting tables, and linked to make floral chains. As we drape a floral garland across the fall of a crisp, white tablecloth for a wedding buffet, or hang a wreath of welcome on the door, it is intriguing to note that while the designs and fashions may change, the concept is as ancient as history, and as relevant now as it ever was.

We tend to reserve the making of garlands, swags, wreaths, and rings for the most celebrated occasions in our lives, for weddings and christenings, Easter and Christmas, and to overlook the many other party-giving times when a ribbon of flowers draped across the garden gate, swags of sun-bleached grasses and seedheads outlining a doorway, or a circlet of summer flowers on a garden

WIRING FRESH FLOWERS

You Will Need

stub wires ● roll of
florists' silver wire ● wire
cutters ● florists' scissors
● gutta percha (floral)
tape ● scissors

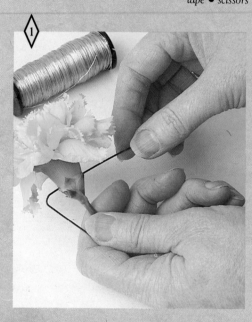

1 To wire a carnation, push a
stub wire horizontally through the
centre of the calyx, until about
7.5cm (3in) of the wire is
exposed.

2 Bring the two ends of the wire
down, parallel to the calyx, and
twist them together beneath it.

3 Wrap one end of a length of
gutta percha (floral) tape around
the calyx, just above the wire.
Twist the flower by holding the
false wire stem in one hand and
the tape in the other. Wrap the
tape around the calyx and false
stem so that each twist overlaps
and sticks to the one before.
Fasten off the tape just above the
end of the false stem.

4 To wire short sprays of flowers
or foliage such as lilac (as shown),
mimosa, or rhododendron, place
one end of a stub wire close to the
short length of stem and bind them
together with silver wire. Wrap the
false stub wire stem with gutta
percha (floral) tape.

5 To wire a leaf such as geranium
(shown here), ivy, or lady's
mantle for inclusion in a posy or
bouquet, thread a stub wire in and
out of the leaf from the stem end
along the central vein, taking very
short 'stitches'. Bind the wire and
the stemlet of the leaf with gutta
percha (floral) tape.

table would enhance the scene.

Floral and foliage garlands are remarkably simple to make. And, on an economical note, since they are almost invariably composed of short-stemmed plant materials, they can utilize clippings left over from larger designs. Side shoots of delphinium cut from long stems arranged in a pedestal design; individual spray chrysanthemum flowers that formed too dense a cluster; florets and leaflets that would come below the water level in a vase – they can all be formed into posies and bound onto a garland with a roll of florists' silver wire.

Most garlands are composed on a central core, which, according to the weight of the plant materials involved, may vary from tightly coiled paper ribbon, thin string, twine, or wire, through cord and plastic-covered wire, to thick rope or even a roll made of wire mesh netting filled with off-cuts of absorbent or dry stem-holding foam. This latter core has the unique advantage, when soaked absorbent foam is used, of providing fresh flowers composed into a garland with a source of moisture. This can be of particular benefit when the garland is to be displayed over several days, over Easter for example.

Most core materials, all the strings, wires, and ropes one might use, are solely utilitarian, and must be considered as an essentially hidden asset to the design. The exception is a new introduction to the core repertoire, called 'paper ribbon', which is available in a wide range of pastel and powerful colours and can, in terms of garland-making, be a positive design advantage. You could, for example, bind a length of orange paper ribbon with intermittent posies of daisies and marigolds, leaving gaps to incorporate the paper core into the design plan. A garland composed along these lines would look pretty draped along a balcony rail, across the front fall of a tablecloth, outlining a porch, looped beneath a window-sill, or twined around a leafless tree branch overhanging a party table. On a note of caution: paper ribbon does not take well to even the slightest shower, so listen to the weather forecast before deciding to use such material for a garden party design.

Other core materials must be densely covered with flowers and foliage so there is no risk of their showing through, or – a favourable option in some cases – first covered in a natural material, such as hay or sphagnum moss, before decorations are added. This method has been chosen for the 'Garland of Evergreens' project, first binding the cord with hay – a highly textural, attractive, and tactile material – before binding on short sprays of

blue pine and bunches of gilded wheat.

Hay and moss wrappings have a special affinity with evergreens and dried materials – a hay-covered swag decorated with bunches of oats and brilliant strawflowers makes a glorious decoration at Halloween or harvest-time – but when fresh flowers are used, such concealment may look clumsy and out of place. To compose a graceful Easter garland to drape across the screen in a church or a midsummer garland of sweet peas and roses to twine around a pole of a tent marquee, the prettiest undercover material is foliage. You can cover the length of the core material with a verdant wrapping of frondy asparagus ferns, trails of small-leafed and variegated ivy, greeny-yellow periwinkle leaves (first given a long drink of water), green and silver lamium, or even bunches of grass. In that way, and with a natural backing to the garland, you can, if you wish, be a little sparing in your use of flowers, and bind on individual blooms or small posies at intervals along the length. On a purely aesthetic note, it is advisable to choose variegated or light-coloured foliage to partner spring and summer flowers, from paper-white narcissus to Peruvian lilies. The deep, dark shades of many evergreens would completely overshadow such flowers, and give the garland an unseasonal and heavy look.

Some plant materials can themselves be used as the core material for a garland, which saves a considerable amount of time in wrapping and binding. Examples are smilax (*Asparagus asparagoides*), which has stemlets of triangular-shaped leaves branching out along a sturdy stem, and hop vines (*Humulus lupulus*), which can be used fresh or dried. For a summer wedding garland you could bind posies of, say, pinks or tiny button carnations, godetia, and gypsophila to the smilax trail, and create a luxurious decoration that belies the speed of its composition. And for an autumn celebration you might want to assemble pom-pom dahlias, zinnias, crab apples and so on, and wire them to the tangled web of a hop vine. The finished garland could be hung around a door or window frame, over a mantelpiece, around the edge of a harvest supper table, or on a pole at ceiling level reaching from side to side of a room corner.

DECORATIVE CIRCLES

Decorative circles have long possessed a deep meaning that reaches far beyond mere adornment. Through the centuries, they have been regarded as symbols of protection, love, friendship, welcome, prosperity, rebirth, and

Bunches of golden wheat, linseed (flaxseed), and grasses are wired onto a rope of thick straw and other materials – poppy seedheads, bunches of cinnamon sticks, wired nuts, and ribbon bows – added at random. The rope makes a seasonal decoration at a harvest festival or Thanksgiving, and can be hung in church, on a door or wall, or on a tree, as here. **Opposite**

A fresh flower circlet can hang in church in the porch, the vestry, or on a screen, or can decorate the reception room for a wedding or christening party. This one is composed of flower posies wired onto a vine wreath form. The flowers include meadowsweet, goldenrod, lady's mantle, sweet peas, Peruvian lilies, and pinks. **Below**

even life itself. And so, drawing on this symbolism, you could compose, for example, a hoop of red roses for your Valentine; a circlet of flowers picked from the garden as a gift for a friend; a wreath of aromatic herbs to welcome a new neighbour; or a dainty ring of sweet peas, lady's mantle, and meadowsweet to decorate the church for a baptism or other occasion.

Most circlets are composed of a central core, although, as with garlands there are exceptions; you can twist and weave supple stems of foliage like clematis or hops into wreaths that are decorative in their own right. You can construct a simple wreath base from supple grass,

Wear it with style or use it as an outdoor table decoration – however it's used, a straw hat ringed with flower posies captures the mood of summer. Give the flowers a long drink of water before binding them to a wire ring, and spray them with a fine mist of cool water. **Right**

It was an old Provençal custom for young girls to wear grass and flower headdresses at midsummer festivals. The notion has other applications, too, and grass rings decorated with fresh or dried flowers make colourful wall or door decorations. **Opposite**

bryony, sheep's parsley (Queen Anne's lace), or other stems, then decorate it with a medley of colourful flowers added at random rather than in symmetrical order. The 'May Day Wreath' project in celebration of the May Day festival in Greece, is composed in this way, with posies and individual flowers bound onto the ring with natural twine, in a spontaneous-looking fashion.

Grass stem rings formed the base for festival headdresses, too, and in provincial France young girls once wore circlets of grasses studded with bright meadow flowers for the midsummer celebrations. This decoration can be adapted for a room: you could hang the grass ring on a door or wall, over a mirror, the back of a chair, or, romantically, on a bedpost.

With the revival of interest in decorative rings, you can now buy a wide variety of wreath bases in florists' shops and department stores. Dried stem rings, vine wreath forms, and twisted or bleached willow rings can all be decorated with posies of fresh flowers and foliage for short-lived decorations, or with dried plant material for long-term display.

A relatively new addition to the wreath-base repertoire is the preformed ring of absorbent stem-holding foam encased in a rigid plastic base, available from florists in a range of sizes. These rings, which provide fresh flowers with a moisture source, can be used throughout the year as wall hangings or table decorations. Outline the ring with periwinkle leaves, fill it with short-stemmed daffodils, tulips, and pansies, and embellish it with a cluster of lighted tapers for an Easter table decoration; cover one with lady's mantle and cornflowers, and stud it with strawberries pierced with cocktail sticks for a midsummer party piece; or define the ring with ivy leaves, fill in with sweet peas, Peruvian lilies, and roses, and cover it with the wedding-veil effect of white-flowered gypsophila.

Foam rings, for all their versatility and usefulness, share one major drawback with other man-made stem-holding materials: they are not fit to be seen. For this reason, it is important to plan your decoration to include an all-concealing cover of an inexpensive and readily available decorative material – it may be a handful of ivy leaves or other foliage, a bunch of sheep's parsley flowers (Queen Anne's lace) you can pick from the wayside, or a bunch of oats – before adding the more precious or scarce components of the arrangement.

A light covering of hay or sphagnum moss can also be used to conceal a base ring. To cover in this way, take handfuls of hay or moss, spread the material over the ring to cover it completely, including both inside and outside rims, and secure it at intervals with U-shaped staples made from half stub wires. Once a ring is covered with sweet-smelling hay, the very essence of summer, there is no need to cover every scrap of the surface with flowers; indeed, any show-through areas can be an attractive part of the design.

FESTIVAL FLOWERS

Every flower arranger's calendar is highlighted throughout the year by the religious and seasonal festivals, times when homes and places of worship have traditionally been adorned with flowers, and when perhaps we feel most inspired and at our most creative. In spring there is the

This colourful Easter arrangement, which represents a garden in springtime, would be a joy for a child to compose. The mimosa, daffodil, narcissus, and ranunculus stems are held in shallow blocks of foam beneath the sphagnum moss. The idea could be adapted to feature other spring flowers such as primulas, grape hyacinth, and miniature tulips. **Right**

Delicate and pretty spring flowers – violets, primroses, and primulas ringed with ivy leaves – are arranged in eggshell containers and displayed in an egg-carrier and pottery egg-cups, to create a seasonal group for an Easter breakfast table. **Opposite**

Easter festival, and the May Day celebrations still adhered to in some country regions. In autumn, harvest festivals, Halloween, and Thanksgiving Day, followed by Christmas and New Year – a wealth of opportunity for anyone who likes to decorate with flowers.

SPRING FESTIVALS

Easter has come to be associated with certain significant colours, which give a strong lead to appropriate decorations. Happily, these colours are yellow, white, and blue, the clear, cool colours of many of the season's prettiest flowers, including daffodils, narcissus, tulips, irises, violets, and primroses.

It is refreshing to arrange Easter flowers in a natural way, just as they grow in the garden or in the wild. You could fit a large, rustic basket with soaked absorbent stem-holding foam, cover the top with a concealing layer of sphagnum moss, and arrange a handful of pussy willow twigs or bare apple branches among which a host of

golden daffodils could 'grow', their stems upright and their flower heads at varying heights. Such a basket could stand in a hallway, the hearth, or a porch, or on the floor or a table in church. On a smaller scale, you could cut a block of soaked foam into a mound and use it to line a woven dish. Cover it with moss – which has a special affinity with this 'indoor garden' style of decoration – and insert trails of variegated ivy and clusters of daffodils, narcissus, ranunculus, and grape hyacinths (*Muscari*), their stems cut short and the flower heads nestling close against the covering of moss.

Children love to help with Easter decorations, especially when they include painted or dyed eggs. A charming way to combine eggs and flowers is to conceal a trio of small water-filled vases among a cluster of decorated eggs in a bowl, and fill the vases with the tiny, delicate flowers of spring – primulas and primroses, aconites (monkshood) and violets. Another notion which appeals to children is to use eggshells as miniature vases. To do this, break each shell close to the top, tip out the egg and wash the shell. Stand a collection of plain or decorated shells in an egg-holder or in separate egg-cups, and fill each with a spring posy of flowers and dainty leaves. To encircle a clutch of eggs with flowers, you could make a floral ring for a table decoration, stand it on a large plate, and fill the centre with moss. Then arrange a 'nest' of eggs on the moss, plain or fancy, chocolate or wrapped, as you and the children please.

May Day, a flower festival with its roots deeply entwined in ancient rites and ceremonies, is a time of special joy for children. If you are asked to 'think flowers' in terms of children's May Day parades, traditional dances and so on, you could make a garland for a young girl to wear by binding daisies to a flexible base – anything from a grass stem ring to a piece of white, plastic-covered wire. These decorations, like large-scale daisy chains, look fresh and pretty whether worn around the neck or on the head. To make a matching headdress, you could bind flowers to a firm wire circle in the way described for the bridesmaid's headdress project illustrated in this book.

In some parts of southern Europe, children carry posies of flowers on poles wrapped with ribbons, a delightful idea for a school May Day parade. You could adapt the design for the bridal posy project, by binding the flowers to the top of a narrow cane, a style carried

with pride by girls and boys at Spanish festivals.

If you decide to give a May Day party, you could emulate the style of the traditional Maypole by creating floral 'torches' to stand in tubs on either side of the door, porch, or archway, in pots on a balcony, or in a patch of garden that may benefit from a temporary injection of colour. To make each decoration, push three or four cylinders of soaked stem-holding foam onto a narrow cane or straight twig – hawthorn was traditional for the English village Maypole – and cover it closely with flowers. Rings of roses, cornflowers, single spray chrysanthemums, and so on, make a powerful impact and a brilliant decoration.

Tie strips of multi-coloured paper ribbons beneath the flowers to hang down and flutter in the slightest breeze around the pole.

AUTUMN FESTIVALS

It is impossible not to marvel at the abundance of crops in this season of mellow fruitfulness; impossible not to be inspired by the rich, warm tones of autumn leaves and berries, the many varieties of chrysanthemum and dahlia, and the wealth of golden fruits, from russet-coloured apples to vibrant pumpkins, that brighten gardens, markets, and shops.

A pottery jug of golden wheat and a family of maize dolls make a simple still-life group appropriate to harvest-time.
Left

Autumn provides a golden opportunity to create colourful displays for harvest festivals. This carved wooden plate is arranged symmetrically with apples, pears, and plums alternated with glossy rosehips.
Below

stems of yellow or orange pyracantha (firethorn) from a friend's garden, and be offered – in the best harvest festival tradition – a box of fruit and vegetables by a neighbour. More than enough food for thought.

To decorate a chest or table you could fit a shallow woven dish or a wooden seed tray or salad bowl with a piece of soaked foam, and compose a diagonal outline of copper beech leaves, wheat, and oats colour-splashed with orange Chinese lanterns (winter cherry) and glossy rosehips, positioning a cluster of contrastingly pale pink roses or pink hydrangea heads in the centre. You might choose to arrange a nosegay of pom-pom chrysanthemums, goldenrod, strawflowers, and sloes in a shallow basket, the stems placed horizontally in a block of foam,

If you are asked to contribute to the team effort of decorating a church for the harvest festival, usually celebrated at the end of September or the beginning of October, there may be a master plan arrived at by mutual agreement, or you may be allocated an area – the pulpit, a south window, or a treasured oak chest – and be invited to carry out your own ideas for the decoration. Your design plan may be influenced by the plant materials you have available or can buy locally, and those offered by friends. You may be able to gather armfuls of yellowing leaves and a bunch of wild oats or wheat in the countryside, cut a basketful of rust-coloured flowers from your garden, a few

as if the materials had just been harvested. Or you might fill a shallow basket to overflowing with an arrangement of produce, a melon and a vegetable marrow, red and green peppers, aubergines (eggplant), a head or two of sweetcorn, a stem of oats, and, as an apparent afterthought, a thick string of dense black elderberries. Baskets of harvest-time produce have a place at the foot of pedestal designs and on tables, steps, and windowsills; wherever, in fact, another inch of space can be found.

Similar decorative arrangements are suitable for the Thanksgiving Day celebrations, when cereals, fruit, and vegetables are prominent among design components. You could compose a garland of wheat and oats decorated with bunches of red and green chillies, tiny aubergines (eggplant) and artichoke heads, and drape it around a pine dresser in the kitchen, the trestle table used for the buffet, or an entrance porch. Or compose a garland of branches of green and yellow, red and russet leaves bound onto a hidden core, and wound around with strings of cranberries threaded onto a flexible wire.

On a smaller scale, and in keeping with both harvest and Thanksgiving traditions, you could make or buy a thick raffia or straw plait and decorate it with handfuls of wired almonds and pecans, bunches of wheat and linseed (flaxseed), large contrasting poppy seedheads, and clusters of raffia-tied cinnamon sticks. Finish the plait with a cluster of ribbon bows, and hang it on a gatepost, door, or even a tree beside the party table. Less substantial plaits, thin enough to be flexible, make beautiful garlands to outline the edge of a table or drape across a tablecloth front. Here, with a core of plaited raffia or straw, is a garland that is already good-looking and needs the minimum of embellishment. Bunches of chillies, clusters of nuts glued together, colourful autumn leaves wired in pairs or trios – the design potential is infinite.

This evergreen wreath is composed on an absorbent foam ring base, which keeps the plant materials looking fresh throughout the long holiday period. Gilded poppy seedheads and small gold baubles provide glittering highlights, matched by the tinsel ribbons. **Opposite**

Celebrate harvest festivals and Thanksgiving with a basket of colourful fruit and vegetables decorated with a shiny-black stem of elderberries. In church, you could place the offering at the foot of a pedestal of flowers, on a bench, a wooden chest, or a deep windowsill. **Below**

Focus attention on a corner of a room or the centre of a Christmas buffet table with a group of cream candles held in a variety of glass containers. Floral additions can be kept to a minimum – three stems of lilies provide an elegant understatement. **Right**

Decorative rings have become a traditional part of North American Thanksgiving celebrations. This is the day – the last Thursday in November – when holiday wreaths of evergreens and other plant materials are first hung on the front door or – an aromatic option – above the fireplace, where the heat of the fire will intensify the warm scent of the pine, fir, and spices. You can change the design, colour, and texture by wiring stems of bay and laurel to a stem base and binding on clusters of scarlet berries; threading alternating kumquats and bay leaves onto a strong wire and – as it is a decoration with double-sided good looks – hang it in a window; compose a herb and spice ring including heads of garlic, dried mushrooms, bunches of fennel, dried marjoram flowers, and unruly raffia bows; or – surely the most appetizing Thanksgiving decoration of all – cover a dry polystyrene foam ring on all its visible sides with cranberries simply pinned in place.

Halloween, which falls between the harvest and Thanksgiving festivals, calls for designs which are perhaps more enchanting than purely decorative, verging even on the bizarre. Taking a cue from the popular All Hallow's Eve game of bobbing or ducking for apples, you could bind uneven and untidy-looking gnarled twigs onto a copper-wire ring frame and decorate it with rosy-red apples and clumps of lichen; dry apple rings (first soaked in acidulated water) in a low-temperature oven and stick them in overlapping circles onto a ring frame; or use hollowed-out apples as unusual candle-holders.

To rival the traditional pumpkin lantern as the centre of attention, you could scoop out a pumpkin shell, fit it with soaked stem-holding foam and arrange an unruly fanburst of twigs, spindle berries, Chinese lanterns (winter cherry), globe thistles, and strawflowers.

Vegetable marrows make remarkable Halloween decorations, too. If you have some past their best, you can scoop out hollows using first an apple corer and then a spoon, and fill some with small phials or pillboxes of water to hold fresh flowers, others with stubby candles in a variety of colours, and still others with thick, forked and twisted twigs.

If, by the time Christmas comes, you have not had a welcome wreath on the front door since Thanksgiving, you might like to consider a range of options based on the various types of ring forms. If your choice is for the traditional circle of evergreens, introduce colour and textural variety by including variegated holly or ivy, spotted laurel or elaeagnus (silver berry), small-leaved box or berberis (barberry), spiky yew or rosemary, and feathery cypress or juniper – the latter if only for its pungent aroma. You can go still further, in design terms, and spray

Hang up a welcome wreath for Christmas. This lavish-looking decoration is composed on a double copper-wire ring frame covered with sphagnum moss. The plant materials, which include hydrangea and purple sage and a rich variety of evergreens, are bound into small bunches and wired to the base. The tartan ribbons not only match the door colour, but add a Victorian feel to the design. **Left**

A fanciful indoor tree makes a decorative alternative to traditional pine. Either use a foam sphere (available from florists) or crush a large piece of wire mesh netting into a ball shape and insert evergreen stems and wired fruits. This tree flourishes with cypress and laurel leaves and bears apples, tangerines, and rosehips. The ivy-entwined cane is firmly secured in a large flowerpot. **Below**

some foliage stems with gold; include bunches of gilded wheat, linseed (flaxseed), and poppy seedheads; wire on small fruits such as kumquats and apples, and gold-splattered nuts and acorns; add dried flowers and foliage such as blue-grey hydrangea bracts and sage leaves; or follow the Victorian tradition and add tiny cotton bags filled with potpourri, miniature wrapped parcels, colourful bon-bons, and even children's trinkets.

Once you have made a Christmas wreath, you are spoilt for choice in the manner of its display. You can hang it vertically on any available wall or door; suspend it horizontally on bright red ribbons (when you will have to cover the underside, too, with evergreen); hang fruits all around the base in true medieval fashion; or use it as a table decoration.

A preformed absorbent foam ring is the ideal platform on which to create a traditional Advent ring, a table-top decoration of evergreens and four candles, one of which is lit on each of the four Sundays of Advent. If you like to use thick candles with a diameter of 2.5 cm (1in) or more, it is best to insert them in plastic candle spikes (available from florists), as the points of these are less likely to break up the foam.

The term 'Christmas tree' is open to more than one interpretation, and it can be refreshing to break with convention and create a round evergreen tree as a table-top or floor-standing decoration. A shoulder-high tree would look good in an alcove or niche, a porch or room corner, or as one of a pair framing an arch or doorway. To hold the stems, you can use a large pre-formed polystyrene sphere (30cm/12in diameter); or make a ball of crumpled wire mesh netting filled, if you wish, with damp sphagnum moss or off-cuts of soaked absorbent foam. Impale the sphere on a bamboo cane or straight twig, wire it securely if it seems likely to slip down, and cover it with short sprays of evergreens – cypress and laurel are striking choices. Once the tree has burst into leaf, you can add any colourful crop of your choice: wired-on fruit such as clementines and apples, rosehips, baubles, decorative birds, and so on. Plant the trunk firmly in an earthenware pot or basket holder, using plaster of Paris or florists' hard-setting clay and a concealing layer of moss or snow-like white polystyrene granules.

MEASURING UP

Whenever you are planning flower arrangements and other compositions, and especially ones that are to set the scene for a festival or public occasion, it is important to start by taking stock of the situation.

If the arrangements are to be in a church or other place of worship, perhaps for a wedding or baptism, ask permission of the preacher and check whether there are any restrictions that might affect your plans. At certain times of year you may not be allowed to place flowers on the altar; in most churches no flower arrangements are permitted during Lent, and some churchmen do not allow any decoration to be placed in or around the font. Once this has been clarified, it is tactful to ask the person who organizes the flower-arranging rota if you may take over the duties for the day in question. Also ask to be shown what equipment is available for you to use.

Many churches have a selection of pedestal stands, the containers that are used with them, and even large pieces of crumpled wire mesh netting, which could cover the foam and give extra security to large designs.

Take a measuring tape, notebook, and pencil with you when you go to the church, public hall, or other venue so that you can make a thorough assessment of the various features. Measure the depth, width, and height of a niche; the depth and width of a windowsill and a bench; the top surface area of a table, chest, or shelf; and the dimensions of a door or fabric drape. When measuring the area to be decorated by a garland, remember to allow for any drapes or curves in the design and for the length of any side trails. If a garland is to be wound around a substantial pillar, the height measurement alone will not be enough. Unless you are a mathematician and can accurately make such calculations, it is best to tape a piece of string to the top of the pillar, wind it around to give the density of the design you require, then measure the string once you have released it.

PREPARING A PEDESTAL

A pedestal, or stand, may be the largest flower arrangement you will be called upon to create, but if you take the preparation stage by stage it should not present any problems.

- *Choose a wide, shallow container such as a discarded baking dish to hold the foam. According to the scale of the arrangement, you may need one whole block of absorbent stem-holding foam standing on end, with half a block, also on end, in front of it.*
- *Press strips of florists' adhesive clay onto the underside of the container, and press the dish firmly to the top of the stand. If you wish, you can fix two plastic prongs to the base of the dish – first making sure it is absolutely dry – with blobs of florists' adhesive clay, then press the two pieces of foam onto the spikes.*
- *If you are planning to use thick stems of foliage or top-heavy stems of, for example, large chrysanthemums which may cause the foam to split, cover it with a piece of wire mesh netting. Do not crumple as if to fit inside the neck of a container, but press it on top of the foam to fit closely over it. Tuck any rough edges inside the rim of the container.*
- *You can use either medium-gauge roll wire or florists' adhesive tape to make doubly sure that the container, foam, and covering wire mesh, if any, stay firmly in place. Tape or wire over and around the foam, the container, and the top of the pedestal, as if taping a package. This extra security measure is especially important when large and heavy plant materials are to be arranged.*
- *If you will need to raise some plant materials more than their natural stem length will allow, you can use plastic or metal cones, which are available at florists, fitted to narrow cones or stout wires. Fit the cones with soaked stem-holding foam – cut it to shape first, then soak it – and hold it in place with criss-crossing strips of narrow florists' adhesive tape. Press the cone 'stilts' into the foam blocks. A large arrangement may need one cone at the centre back, two at a similar level facing to either side, and two at the sides. The stand is now ready for the arrangement. If time is short on the day of the event, it may be a good idea to prepare the stand or stands to this stage a day or so in advance.*

Make a careful assessment of the background against which each arrangement will be viewed. Will a flower stand be seen against a brick wall, a red curtain, or pale stone? Will it be placed in a dark corner that is beyond the reach of the sun's rays and scarcely benefits from the electric light? Will a stand have to fit into a narrow niche, where a generous, flowing design might seem cramped? Will a garland that is to be draped across a screen have to compete with ornately decorated wood?

All set for a wedding or christening – a wall niche decorated with a gently curving arrangement of stocks, gerberas, and spray chrysanthemums with hosta (plantain lily) leaves at the base to give visual weight and conceal the stem-holding material. **Left**

An appraisal of these factors can help you design your arrangements so that they will be seen to best advantage. An arrangement that will be viewed against the sometimes strongly geometric pattern of a brick wall may benefit from a clearly-defined outline, such as a rim of foliage. One that is to be placed in front of fabric should, as far as possible, both tone with the material and follow the overall colour scheme of the occasion. If, for example, the background is red silk and the bride has chosen yellow, then you could compromise by placing mid-toned yellow flowers at the heart of the arrangement, where

they will be seen as the focal points, and taking pale cream and pale pink flowers – two-toned Peruvian lilies, for example – out to the sides. If the flowers will be seen against a pale stone background, which could make a largely pastel-coloured arrangement look washed out, use dark and well-defined foliage for the outline and draw the eye to the centre of the design with a cluster of flowers in deep, rich tones.

Your choice of plant material will also be affected by the strength and direction of the natural or artificial light by which each arrangement will be seen. If a design will

be viewed in strong light – as one on a south-facing windowsill would be – it is best to avoid both pale pastel colours, which would appear faded, and deep shades such as ruby red and purple, which would look almost black. Conversely, an arrangement placed in the far recesses of a church should combine both pale and middle tones, if it is to have any chance of brightening that dark corner. A composition of all-white, cream, or pastel-coloured flow-ers, without the definition it would receive in a good light, would appear simply as a shape – a mass of flowers lacking detail. Where a garland is concerned, an ornate background presents the greatest challenge. This could be met, perhaps, by a trail of smilax decorated with large flowers with well-defined shapes – individual gladioli or large, single spray chrysanthemums, for example – or by a garland of, say, lime-green cypress wired with full, round-ed roses or mid-sized dahlias.

Armed with the vital statistics of the situation, you will be able to choose your containers, plan the scale of your arrangements and work out the number of flowers you will need for each. It is a good idea, especially for inexperienced arrangers, to make a sketch of each design, both to help with the 'shopping list' of plant material and for reference when composing the arrangement. Using a different coloured pencil or felt-tipped pen for each plant type, draw the outline of foliage, then the slender flowers or buds that will reach the tips of the design; next, the fully-rounded flowers that will form the central, focal point; and lastly, the filling-in material. Make several sketches, altering the line and balance of the design until you achieve one you find pleasing. If it looks right on paper, there is every chance that it will look just as good in reality.

Roses, aquilegia, and marguerites compose an informal triangular arrangement to decorate a church window for a wedding or christening. The white and pale yellow flowers are seen to advantage against the shadowy corners of the stone. **Left**

PLANNING AN ARRANGEMENT ON A STAND

Arranging flowers on a stand or pedestal offers just as much opportunity as a smaller arrangement to display your creative style. At Eastertime you might choose to arrange a dome of pussy willow branches with an armful of daffodils in a casual way that brings to mind flowers growing in an orchard; a wedding may inspire you to create a display using nothing but trusses of mock orange blossom; at harvest-time or Thanksgiving you might elevate a basket of autumn leaves, Michaelmas daisies (wild asters), and russety fruits to stand in front of the altar.

By tradition, however, there is a certain formality associated with pedestal design. Furthermore, many arrangers, especially those new to the art, find it easier to compose a pedestal design based on recognized outlines, usually a triangle or asymmetrical triangle, using plant materials in three specific shapes. These are known as 'points', for the outlines and extremities of the design; 'rounds', for the focal point and heart of the arrangement; and 'flats', to cover the mechanics and flower stems.

Whether you are following the outlines of one of the arrangements illustrated here or have sketched your own design, select plant materials carefully so you have some straight stems for the uprights and others that naturally curve (both to the right and left) for the sides. If you are arranging a pair of stands, be sure your material will allow you to compose two 'mirror image' designs when the material is divided in two.

As a general guide to planning how much plant material you will need, here is a suggested list for a triangular stand design, which may measure 100cm (40in) from the top of the stand to the tip of the arrangement, and about the same from side to side:

- **Foliage branches:** *allow seven, one for the centre back, one just in front of it, one on either side, one flowing outwards and downwards on either side, and one flowing outwards and downwards at the front*
- **'Flat' foliage:** *allow eight to ten leaves, such as bergenia, hosta (plantain lily), or ivy, to hide the mechanics*
- **'Pointed' flowers:** *allow five or seven (always an uneven number). Gladioli, antirrhinum, and lilac are good examples*
- **'Round' flowers:** *allow five or seven for the central position. Cabbage roses, hydrangea, peonies and carnations, among others, would be suitable*
- **Fillers:** *it is helpful to have sprays of materials such as flowering shrubs, lady's mantle, or spiraea to act as fillers*

WEDDING DESIGNS

A wedding is perhaps the most significant occasion of all, not only for the bride and groom but for anyone entrusted with setting the floral scene. The colours you choose for the flowers will form part of the overall scheme chosen by the bride, with, it is hoped, allowances being made for seasonal availability.

Whether the bride's preference is for the soft, flattering tints of peaches and cream, the clear tones of yellow and green, or for deep anemone shades of purple and pink, it is a good idea to have one consistent flower type linking all the arrangements. You could take gypsophila, with its pretty mass of bridal-white florets, as the link in the floral chain. You might decide to compose a pedestal arrangement (more usually, and less dauntingly, called a 'stand') for the entrance porch, and a pair of matching stands on either side of the altar, with a veil of gypsophila surrounding the principal flowers. A table or chest at the back of the nave or in a side aisle could be decorated with a cloud of gypsophila alone, in a basket or glass bowl; and windowsill arrangements, which should have strong, clearly defined silhouettes, could have massed sprays of the tiny white flowers clustered around the focal point. You might like to outline the window ledges with trails of greenery decorated at intervals with bunches of gypsophila and one or two feature flowers, and to hang posies of similar flowers on the ends of the front pews.

Other flowers that could be used in a similar way include sheep's parsley, or Queen Anne's lace, which forms a misty white ribbon along roadsides in springtime, and lady's mantle, with its minute, yellow-green flowers. This plant, well worth growing for its versatility in arrangements, blends well with flowers of every other colour, and lends a pretty country-style look to the most formal arrangements.

Flowers for the centre of a buffet table need not be formal in style. This design, which would be charming for a wedding reception, is composed of catkins, eucalyptus, daffodils, narcissus, and roses arranged in a rustic basket. A posy of freesia and mimosa is wired to the point of the ribbon garland. **Opposite**

REMINDER LIST

When you are going to arrange flowers on site, be it in a church, public hall, or meeting room, it is best to be on the safe side and take with you everything you will need. Here is a checklist to help you prepare your portable flower-arranging kit:

- **Foliage,** *already conditioned in water, stem ends split or crushed, lower leaves stripped off. Take foliage flat, in boxes, or upright in a container such as a bucket.*
- **Flowers,** *prepared as for foliage*
- **Plastic sheet** *and/or* **newspaper** *to cover the working area (floor or work surface)*
- **Secateurs (pruning shears)**
- **Florists' scissors**
- **Container** *such as shallow dish, urn, bowl, or basket (unless suitable ones available at venue)*
- **Absorbent stem-holding foam,** *soaked in water, transported in sealed plastic bag or lidded plastic box*
- **Piece of wire mesh netting** *to cover foam for large arrangement (unless available at venue)*

- **Plastic prongs** *to secure foam, pinholders, etc.*
- **Roll of medium-gauge wire** *to attach container to a pedestal*
- **Roll of florists' adhesive clay**
- **Roll of florists' adhesive tape**
- **Scissors**
- **Metal or plastic cones** *to raise height of materials*
- **Kitchen cloth** *or* **paper towels** *to wipe up spills*
- **Large plastic bag** *to bring home cut-off stems and other unwanted materials*
- **Dustpan and brush**
- **Fine-mist water spray** *or* **plant mister**
- **Container of water** *if none is available on site*
- **Reference** *for the arrangements you are planning*
- **Ribbons**
- **Appropriate fixing materials** *for garlands, swags, pew end arrangements, etc.*
- **Accessories,** *for instance, fruit, preserves, and loaves of bread for harvest displays*

A pedestal arrangement to decorate a church for a wedding or christening. The framework of the foliage marks the outlines of the triangular shape and serves as filling material between the flowers. The cluster of rhododendron flowers and hosta (plantain lily) leaves forms the focal point, slightly recessed at the heart of the design. **Left**

A floral hoop is a charming way to carry bridal flowers. The hoop is made of flexible cane bound into a circle and covered with white ribbon and yellow bows. The flowers and ming foliage are gathered into posies and left in water until shortly before the event. Then they are bound onto the hoop with silver roll wire. **Below**

Ideally, arrangements for the reception room should echo those at the ceremony in some way. It may be that the church, where space is rarely a consideration, was decorated with arrangements composed mainly of pale pink lilies, peonies, and roses, but this floral combination may be out of scale with the more confined space of a reception room. It may be possible, in that case, to compose a stand close to the door similar to those in the church, and to translate the flower combination by using a mixture of roses and the smaller Peruvian lilies in a similar colour for arrangements on the top table and guests' tables.

Flowers for the bride and her attendants to carry and wear may present a different challenge to the arranger, as well as a wide choice of style options. Young bridesmaids may carry a simple posy of flowers of the type a child might pick for herself: a bunch of daisies tightly tied with blue and white gingham ribbon; a clutch of pink, blue, and white cornflowers tied with the narrowest of ribbons in those colours; or a small basket of primroses and violets. The posy shown later in these pages, illustrated with step-by-step photographs, is a development of this kind of sweet simplicity, and a style which looks attractive regardless of the angle at which a young bridesmaid might choose to hold it.

Other posy styles, bouquet designs, and floral head-dresses involve one of a number of wiring techniques. Once binding a short stem or individual floret onto a stub wire and twirling it in your fingers to wrap it with all-concealing gutta percha (floral) tape becomes a matter of reflex action, you have the key to creating a wide variety of designs. These include Victorian-style posies composed of concentric rings of flowers and foliage;

shower bouquets, in which flowers at graduated heights form a delightful cascade; and other arrangements in which the flexible wire stems allow flowers to be angled in a way not possible with natural stems. The project for a bridal bouquet of orchids, Peruvian lilies, and roses is an example of this design flexibility, with the false stems of the roses and mimosa sprays angled so that the flowers thrust outwards, close to the grip.

An added advantage of wiring flowers for a bouquet, and one which increases in direct proportion to the number of woody stems included in the design, is that of circumference. A handful of thin-gauge stub wires discretely wrapped with tape and bound with ribbon is more elegant and comfortable to hold than a thick bunch of wayward twigs!

On the other hand, wired plant materials are irretrievably severed from any source of moisture, and therefore need extra cosseting both before and after being arranged. This is not the time to rush out into the garden at the last minute and cut a handful of roses for a headband; it is far too risky. Gather all the flowers and foliage you will need a day before you plan to arrange them. Cut off unwanted leaves, split or crush the stem ends to facilitate the maximum water intake, and stand them deep in cool water in a cool, shady place overnight. In very hot weather, change the water once or twice as it becomes tepid. When you have completed the design, spray the flowers with a fine mist of cool water and keep it in a cool, dark place, even in the refrigerator. Spray the flowers with more water every few hours, and again on the journey in hot weather.

PARTY PIECES

Flowers have a leading role to play whenever you invite guests to your home, whether it is for a special anniversary party, a high-powered dinner party, or an informal get-together in the garden. It is not usually possible to redecorate the room for the occasion, splash out and buy a new dinner set, or coax the garden into a sudden blaze of colour, but it is possible to enhance the setting with imaginative and effective flower displays.

ANNIVERSARIES

If the party is in celebration of a wedding anniversary, the occasion itself can give you a cue for appropriate flowers and containers. Cotton denotes the first anniversary, and could be represented by crisply starched broderie anglaise

The perfect link between indoor and outdoor living – a jug arranged with a profusion of hedgerow blossoms and stocks, lilacs, roses, carnations, and pinks. Place the arrangement beside an open window and the mingled floral scents will seem to be wafting in from a lavishly-stocked herbaceous border. **Opposite**

(embroidered eyelet) bows tied around a pair of tall vases, or by a piece of the same material covering a bulbous-shaped glass or china container and tied around the rim in a pretty bow. Paper, for the second year, might be incorporated by paper ribbon bows in any of a multitude of colours tied around baskets and boxes, jugs and mugs. A leather jewellery box or tankard would make a striking and unusual container for the third, leather anniversary; while the fourth makes use of fruits and flowers. The 'Christmas Cheer' project, designed as a yuletide celebration, offers plenty of scope for adaption; you could substitute bunches of black and white grapes for the cascades of lychees and pecans. Wood marks the fifth year of marriage, and in recognition of this milestone you might like to arrange flowers in a slatted basket, threading ribbon, raffia, or aromatic stems such as lavender or thyme in and out of the uprights, or compose an arrangement on a wooden board or tray. Five sprays of pink Singapore orchids, five coral roses, and five lilies would underline the significance of the occasion.

Other anniversaries provide other design guidelines. For a 15th-year party, when crystal is the theme, you could arrange a fragrant mound of cabbage and damask roses in a crystal rose bowl; stand a pair of crystal candlesticks in floral circles of sweet peas, feverfew, and cornflowers; or float rose petals in cool, clear water in a glass bowl to mark the occasion.

A silver wedding anniversary, marking 25 years of marriage, might be the occasion for a large party. You could decorate the buffet table with drapes of silver ribbon and pin posies of white, cream, and pale pink flowers on the corners. Assuming the lack of a silver rose bowl or fruit bowl as the centre-piece, you could arrange flowers in a large, square, and absolutely pristine biscuit or cookie tin – surprisingly effective when spilling over with exotic blooms like orchids and stephanotis interspersed with the glint of silver honesty and the softening effect of hare's-tail grass. If the occasion is a more intimate one, marked by a dinner party for a small number of guests, you could

arrange the dinner table flowers in a silvered urn like the one in the 'Note of Formality' arrangement, or flatter each guest with his or her own nosegay at each place setting, the flowers arranged in silver goblets or an assortment of christening mugs.

Another 25 years on, flowers for a golden wedding anniversary could be arranged in a large glass jug or vase fitted with a foam-holding saucer and filled with gold foil sweet papers or candy wrappers (the family's cooperation in the preceding weeks is assured!), or a cylindrical container wrapped around with strips of gold sequin trim. Flowers in white and yellow blended with bunches of gilded wheat and linseed (flaxseed), poppy seedheads, and gold-splashed foliage trails say it all.

Dining-table flowers have a delicate, dual role to play. They should be showy enough to be the centre of decorative attention before the first course arrives, yet not so flamboyant that they detract attention from the food during the course of the meal. And there's yet another balancing act: a table arrangement has to be large enough to be in proportion to the table area as a whole – a honey jar of buttercups and daisies in the centre of a trestle table might well be lost on those people seated at either end – yet not so tall it becomes an obstacle to conversation across the table.

FORMAL FLOWERS

For a formal occasion, you could opt for a fully coordinated look and select a container from a spare piece of china from the dinner set – a vegetable dish, soup tureen, or gravy boat, for example – or a teapot from a matching tea set. If every last piece of the dinnerware is pressed into service, you could use a dish or bowl in one of the colours of the china pattern, picking out the deep green of the leaf design or the rich brown of a Greek key pattern, for instance. Or turn to the timeless elegance of silver, crystal, or cut glass to add sparkle to your design.

Flowers in pastel tints, white, or harmonizing colours are considered to have the most formal pedigree. A white soup tureen fitted with a mound of crumpled wire mesh netting and cascading with lime-green cymbidium orchids, white and yellow ranunculus, and variegated periwinkle leaves would leave a lasting impression of stylish simplicity. A glass fruit bowl prepared in a similar way and arranged with grey-green ballota, pink and peach Shirley poppies, and pink and white stocks would look every inch a country classic.

Colour restraint is less important when you are planning flowers for a buffet table. On this occasion the flowers need to be of sufficient stature to command attention across a crowded room, and to hold their own on a table crowded with food. You could arrange a tall, cylindrical glass vase with a bunch of burgeoning horse-chestnut branches or catkins which, in colour terms, would represent a cool option; or fill a deep bowl with a mass of flowers of a single type. According to the time of the year and the theme of the party, these could be purple irises, scarlet poppies, or an irresistible blend of pastel and white gerberas. Or you could go for bold, and arrange flowers of all shapes, sizes, and colours of the rainbow in one glorious display. An arrangement of this type owes more to the mood of the party than to the colours and style of the surrounding decor. Unless you really want to dazzle guests with colour overstatement, the secret is to

Cheerful informality characterizes a centre-piece for a children's party. The flower holders – cola cans – are fitted with soaked stem-holding foam and fizzing with spray chrysanthemums and spray carnations in the red and white trade-mark colours. **Left**

What could be prettier or more romantic than a cluster of pastel-pink roses, Shirley poppies, and geraniums in a hand-painted mug. A design like this would set the scene for strawberries and cream in the garden. **Right**

with a burst of daffodils or anemones; or make a design using three cola cans fizzing over with flowers in the red and white brand image.

When you are planning a party for young children, toys open up another range of possibilities, though check first that your choice of container does not form part of the young host's game plan. A wooden train or truck can have a bright new cargo of orange and blue spring flowers or red and yellow autumn ones; a small wooden cradle makes a pretty centre-piece when filled with roses and gypsophila; while a set of plastic beakers in bright reds, blues, and yellows makes a brilliant vase group no matter what flowers they display.

OUTDOOR ENTERTAINING

Flower arrangements for a party held in the garden must meet a number of criteria, some determined by climate. This is the perfect opportunity to compose designs in the complementary colour pairing of blue and orange or yellow and mauve, which will both hold their own against strong competition for a deep blue sky and blazing sun, or

blend some pastels and mid-tones with the deep reds and bright yellows, to bridge the colour gap.

CHILDREN'S PARTIES

Children's parties offer a similar no-holds-barred approach to floral art, and a chance to look beyond the usual range of containers, however wide that may be. In fact, the containers may well take the lead, requiring only the minimum of plentiful or inexpensive flowers to complete the design. Food and drink cans and packets, so familiar to children of all ages, make good if controversial talking points among a peer group sure to have their own brand preferences. You could line three colourful cardboard sweet packets or candy boxes with foil or plastic, fit them with soaked stem-holding foam, and fill each with a different colour of strawflower or cornflower; line a fast-food chicken or burger box in a similar way, and fill it

provide a welcome patch of brilliance against grey clouds. Pastel colours, which can look either washed out or lack-lustre in extreme daytime conditions, are a better choice for an evening party, when a shallow glass bowl brimming over with pink and white heathers and pink and cream ranunculus and roses will continue to glow warmly long after the shades of evening have fallen.

Containers, too, should be selected with an eye on the weather. On the better-safe-than-sorry principle, it is best to avoid tall, slender, or unstable holders when there is a risk of a stiff breeze. If you do use a tall container such as a wine carafe as a pedestal conversion, weigh it first with a heavy and if it is glass, presentable ballast.

A party in the garden is the perfect occasion for a flurry of garlands and swags – floral ribbons draped around the buffet table, across an exterior wall, over a door, or twined around a tree trunk. If the party is quite formal, you could develop the string of posies theme and attach tiny posies like floral polka-dots at random across the front vertical fall of the buffet tablecloth or the corners of separate tables. Make each posy of three or four stems of feverfew, cornflowers, lady's mantle, and marguerites, tie the stems with the narrowest of ribbons, and leave them in water as long as possible. Just before the party, dry the

Slices of juicy watermelon emphasize the exotic colour blend of the flower pyramid, a design that would look equally stunning in a conservatory or as the centre of attention on a table in the garden. **Opposite**

A casual arrangement to decorate a garden for a wedding reception or a springtime party – the large jug is filled to overflowing with wayward stems of sheep's parsley (Queen Anne's lace) and then arranged with vibrant pink gerberas and campion. **Left**

A friend who does not have a garden would especially welcome the gift of a free-style posy. This one, which has a refreshing blend of aromas, is composed of lemon balm and marguerites, with clusters of fennel seedheads close to the grip. **Left**

A herb ring bearing the scents and colours of a summer garden would make a thoughtful housewarming gift with lingering appeal. The base, a double copper-wire ring frame covered with sphagnum moss, is decorated with densely-packed bunches of lavender, marjoram, cornflowers, sage, pinks, and fennel – materials which will dry satisfactorily in a dry, airy room to compose a long-lasting wall decoration. **Opposite**

stems and attach the posies to the cloth with florists' adhesive clay. You could arrange slightly larger but matching posies in containers to decorate each table.

Gift days

The tradition of giving flowers to friends, loved ones, and visiting guests has its origins in the ancient world, and has lost none of its freshness and charm since.

You might like to present flowers to your partner to mark St Valentine's Day; to your mother on her special day; to the proud parents in celebration of a baby's birth or baptism; to friends or neighbours as a house-warming gesture; as a birthday or anniversary gift; or simply to say 'thank you'. And when you have chosen and arranged the flowers yourself, then the gift becomes all the more meaningful, and more pleasurable to receive.

If you must take the flowers on a longish journey, a basket arrangement is ideal. You can buy inexpensive baskets in ethnic and charity shops and paint them in toning colours; weave slatted baskets with ribbons or raffia; bind the handle with ribbon or trails of leaves; or trim the basket rim with lace or paper doilies. There is no end to their versatility. Or make the basket an even more significant part of the gift by choosing a more substantial one with a long and industrious after-life, as a holdall for toiletries, knitting wools, sewing sundries, and so on. Baskets are easy to carry, will not break in transit, and can be fitted with soaked stem-holding foam.

The project for a Mother's Day gift basket is an example of how pretty such an arrangement can be. The basket is painted in toning colours, holding a lightly scented blend of roses, Peruvian lilies, and eucalyptus.

As a gift for a flat- or apartment-dwelling friend you could arrange a basket of garden flowers like sweet peas, poppies, and spurge, or an aromatic blend of flowering herbs, such as marjoram and sage, sweet cicely and chives. And for someone taking charge of a new garden – or just installing a window box – you could compose a *pot et fleur* in a lined basket, combining small pots of herbs with clusters of marigolds and garden pinks or button carnations arranged in soaked foam.

Posies, ready-made arrangements the recipient just puts in water, present an equally attractive gift option. Unless you know the person's colour preferences, it is best to keep to 'safe' colours such as cream, white, and all the pastels, since a bunch of bold, red carnations might strike a discordant note with a visiting speaker's outfit or furnishing scheme. Even if it is to mark the most formal of occasions, a gift posy can have a charming simplicity. A cascade of daisies and sweetly scented lemon balm tied with a strip of white net; a shower of heathers and hellebores tied with green and pink ribbons; a creamy-white composition of stephanotis, freesias, and spray carnations tied together with green and white gingham: there are so many ways of saying it with flowers.

RAISED ALOFT

You might have been asked to arrange a pedestal in church for Easter or a spring wedding, or at a public hall for a formal reception. Or you might like to compose a floral design on a stand to decorate the hall or a corner of a room for a special party. This design combines some of the loveliest blossoms and flowers of the season, in the traditional colours of the Easter festival.

You Will Need

pedestal stand • florists' adhesive clay • scissors • 2 plastic prongs • absorbent stem-holding foam, cut to shape and then soaked • narrow florists' adhesive tape or roll of medium-gauge wire • wire cutters • flowers and blossoms such as mimosa, lilac, lilies, and narcissus • foliage such as eucalyptus and flowering shrub • branches of pussy willow and catkins • secateurs (pruning shears)

1 The wrought-iron pedestal stand used for this design, with an adjustable stem, is already fitted with a dish-shaped metal container to hold stem-holding foam. If you use one which has a flat top, and requires an additional waterproof container, you can prepare it using the method described earlier.

3 Position sprays of lilac to follow the outline of the eucalyptus, one tall straight stem to reinforce the central height and others flowing outwards and downwards at the centre and sides. Position sprays of mimosa within the triangular shape.

2 Cut two short lengths of adhesive clay and press onto the underside of the two plastic prongs. Press these onto the base of the container, one to the back and one to the front of the centre point. Press two blocks of foam onto the prongs. Tape or wire over the foam and onto the container, parcel

fashion, for extra security. Begin the outline of the triangular shape by positioning long stems of eucalyptus at the centre back and sides. Arrange stems of flowering shrub throughout the design, to form a natural-looking background for the flowers.

4 Arrange stems of lily in bud to
follow the points of the design,
and fully-opened flowers at the centre,
to create visual weight and interest.

5 Fill in the design with narcissus
arranged in clusters. Add short
sprays of mimosa as fillers, and a few
short sprays of pussy willow and catkins
to link the design with the countryside
in spring.

DAFFODIL WOOD

This Easter arrangement evokes one of the loveliest harbingers of spring – the sight of golden daffodils making a bright floral carpet under the bare branches of an apple tree. A piece of twisted and gnarled vinewood represents the tree, and the flowers and the twigs are positioned vertically, as if growing naturally. The arrangement could be positioned in a church porch, on the floor, or on a low wooden chest.

1 If you are not fortunate enough to find a shapely piece of wood in the countryside, it may be available from some florists' shops. As an alternative, to give the impression of a barren tree, you could use a handful of gnarled twigs – apple would be ideal – placed close together, the forked twigs facing in all directions.

2 Place the plate or other solid waterproof liner in the tray. Cut two strips of adhesive clay and press them onto the underside of the plastic prongs. Press them in position well apart on the liner, where they will anchor the main blocks of foam. Press two large pieces of foam onto the spikes and cut other pieces to fill in the circle around the edges. Cut a hole in the foam, towards the back and at one side, and push the vinewood into it. Twist two or three stub wires around the wood, twist the ends and press them at different angles into the foam, so that the 'tree' is held firmly in place.

3 Cover the foam with a thin layer of moss. Scrape away just enough of the moss to expose small areas, and press the daffodil stems vertically into the foam. Cut them to slightly varying heights to give the most natural effect.

4 Cut shorter stems of narcissus and
arrange them in a group in front of
the daffodils. Position stems of ivy to
twine around the vinewood and trail
through a clump of daffodils.

5 Position short sprays of ivy around
the rim to edge and enclose the
design and arrange a few stems with
catkins to provide shape and texture
variation.

MAY DAY WREATH

You Will Need

a handful of supple grass or other stems; you could use sheep's parsley (Queen Anne's lace) or bryony ● florists' scissors ● green binding twine ● scissors ● selection of flowers such as marigolds, cornflowers, spray chrysanthemums, roses, and irises ● small-leafed sprays of foliage, such as box ● roll of florists' silver wire

It's an old Greek custom to hang a colourful floral wreath, a *stefani*, on the door in celebration of the May Day festival. The decorations are composed of rings made of grass or other supple stems bound with a medley of wild and garden flowers. It is an idea well worth adopting for any occasion – just think what a warm welcome a flower ring would signal to party guests.

1 In the Greek tradition, the ring is composed of flower posies selected and arranged at random, not carefully matched and arranged symmetrically. Try to include some wild flowers if available. If the stems you cut to make the ring are too rigid to shape into a circle, soak them in water, then hang them in a bunch to dry.

2 Cut the stems to the length you require. This ring is 30cm (12in) diameter, made of stems 100cm (40in) long. Gather them into a neat bundle and pull out any which are particularly wayward. Wrap the twine around the stems, tie it into a knot and bind it over and around them. Overlap the ends to form a circle and bind securely, tying the twine and cutting off the end.

3 Sort the flowers into groups, those which will be bound into posies and others which will be added individually. Mix and match the flowers for the posies to give the most colourful and informal effect. Cut short the stems of the posy flowers and foliage and bind them with roll wire.

4 Using green twine or silver wire, bind on at random the flower posies and the individual flowers, so that the heads of each posy or separate flower head cover the stems and binding of the one before. It is not necessary to conceal every scrap of the stem ring, since it is a natural and authentic component of the design.

5 Continue binding on flowers to complete the colourful circle. Display it on a door, gate, or an internal or external wall.

VALENTINE TOKEN

For generations red roses have symbolized true love and red rosebuds, a traditional Valentine gift, young and ardent love. This arrangement composed in a heart-shaped basket, is the perfect way to 'say it with flowers'. Use the design as a table decoration when you are dining *à deux*, or give it as a meaningful token. A child's Valentine offering might include a posy of carnations and anemones.

1 Buy the roses at least a day before they are to be arranged, strip off the lower leaves, split the stem ends, and stand them in cool water. Select a variety of foliage, long sprays such as eucalyptus to outline the design, lightweight ming – or asparagus or maidenhair fern – as a filler, and heart-shaped leaves such as geranium to conceal the stem-holding foam.

3 Cut the stems of the roses and rosebuds to different lengths, and cut or split the stem ends so that the flowers will be able to take up water more readily. Position more rosebuds within the outline of the foliage.

2 Stick a small piece of adhesive clay to the base of the waterproof container; a small plastic pot is ideal. Press the holder to the base of the basket, close to the top on one side. Press the piece of soaked foam into the container; the foam should extend at least 1.5cm (½in) above the rim of the basket. Position the eucalyptus stems to outline the design – an irregular triangle – and position the rosebuds to follow those lines.

4 The pink roses, almost fully open, give the design a soft and more feminine appeal. Position the flowers among the red rosebuds, where their shape and colour contrast will be most significant.

5 Fill in the arrangement with more foliage, and place geranium leaves to cover every trace of the foam. The child's posy, a simple bunch of red anemones and carnations, is prettily tied with a scrap of lace trimming.

MOTHER'S DAY BASKET

What could be a more delightful surprise for a mother on her special day than a basket of roses and lilies, arranged with style and sent with love? The basket, painted to tone with the flowers, becomes a permanent keepsake. It would be ideal to hold wools, sewing materials, or bath preparations.

1 As the basket is so much part of the gift, choose a decorative one with care. The basket illustrated, with woven, twisted cane, was painted in uneven stripes of pink gloss paint, to add a touch of sparkle to the arrangement. This colour is repeated in the floral-printed paper ribbon bow, a flamboyant finishing touch to the design.

3 Arrange the roses to make a gently rounded shape, alternating the colours, pink and cream, so that each complements the other.

2 Put the liner in the basket and place the block of foam in it. Cut two strips of adhesive tape and criss-cross them over the foam and down onto the sides of the basket, to hold the foam firmly in place. Arrange the tallest stems of foliage to make a fan shape at the back of the basket. Cut progressively shorter stems for the centre and front, positioning them so they droop and trail over the rim.

4 Add the Peruvian lilies, cutting some individual flowers on short stems and positioning them close against the foam. Fill in the gaps with short sprays of flowering shrub.

5 Unfurl the twisted paper ribbon by pulling it out gently from one end. You need about 1m (1 yard) to make a full, generous bow.

6 Cut the length of ribbon required and tie it into a bow. Ease the loop until neat, and trim the ribbon ends by cutting them at a slant. Thread the stub wire through the back of the loop, twist and insert the two ends into the foam at the front of the basket. Spray the flowers with a fine mist of cool water, and keep the foam moist before you deliver your surprise gift.

HALLOWEEN HIGHLIGHT

You Will Need

piece of twisted vinewood, driftwood, or other well-shaped branch ● well-shaped, forked apple or other twigs, preferably covered with lichen ● small quinces, or golden apples or pears ● clear quick-setting glue or hot glue ● stub wires ● wire cutters ● small waterproof dish ● slice cut from a cylinder of absorbent stem-holding foam, soaked in water ● flowers such as single spray chrysanthemums ● pyracantha (firethorn) berries ● foliage such as ivy and berberis (barberry) ● florists' scissors ● secateurs (pruning shears) ● 2 apples ● apple corer ● 2 candles

Heighten the party atmosphere and brighten the buffet table with a forest of ideas for Halloween. This creation – which can be extended to any length desired – comprises a piece of gnarled and twisted wood, a bunch of apple twigs, and a small harvest of quinces. Add a handful of golden flowers, berries, and leaves and a couple of golden candlesticks, and you are all set to turn the lights down low.

1 To create the effect appropriate to Halloween, select the wood, twigs, and leaves with care. The more gnarled, twisted, forked, and green-encrusted the branches the better; the more purple and veined the ivy leaves, the more spooky the effect will be.

2 Begin by attaching the fruit to the twigs. You can do this in one of two ways, by gluing or wiring. If you decide to use glue, attach the fruits where the twigs fork and there is the largest area of contact. Cover the twig with glue or hot glue, press on the fruit and hold it in place for a few seconds until the glue sets.

3 If you prefer to wire on the fruits, push a stub wire through the back of each one, bring the two wire ends together and twist them firmly. Wrap the wire around a twig and twist the fruit until it rests neatly on the surface.

4 When you have given all the twigs a bountiful fruit crop, position them behind the horizontal branch. Glue the twigs to the wood and secure them in place with stub wires, if necessary, as the weight of the fruit makes the twigs top-heavy. Place the slice of foam in the holder and arrange a 'forest' of twigs and foliage stems, some positioned vertically and others horizontally, on either side.

5 Cut short sprays of the chrysanthemums and some separate flowers and arrange them in the foam. Add sprays of the autumn leaves – berberis (barberry) in this design – and more ivy leaves. The largest ones may be used to conceal the foam. Snip off any flowers that look too crowded or confusing.

6 Position the flower group at one end of the 'fallen branch' where it continues the line of the wood. Use an apple corer to scoop out the centre of the apples and insert a candle in each one. Keep lighted candles away from children or pets.

HARVEST-TIME

It's the time of the year when the gardens, markets, and florists' shops are brimming over with flowers in all the glorious colours of autumn, a time to fill homes and churches with a wonderful profusion of flowers. This design is for a small pedestal decorated with golden yellow, orange, and russet-brown flowers and foliage.

1 If you do not have access to a pedestal, you can compose the arrangement to stand on a small wine table or other occasional table. You could use foliage preserved in glycerin solution instead of the more brittle autumn leaves.

3 Balance the outline – and the weight of the arrangement – by positioning some foliage branches and flowers at the back. Cut thick stems at an angle, slant-wise, so that they can be inserted more easily into the foam. Build up the design by placing spray chrysanthemums to follow the triangular shape.

2 Stick strips of adhesive clay to the underside of the plastic container, and press it firmly onto the pedestal. Position the soaked foam in the container – the one used here has an indent purpose-made to fit the rectangular shape. Secure the foam and container to the pedestal by taking two strips of adhesive tape from side to side and front to back, sticking the ends under the platform of the pedestal. Begin by positioning foliage branches and goldenrod to make the triangular outline of the design.

4 Arrange some of the stems so that the flowers thrust forwards and downwards and trail below the top of the pedestal. It is especially important for large arrangements such as this to have a three-dimensional effect.

5 Position the lilies in the centre front of the arrangement, where they will become the focal point. Arrange roses, an attractive shape contrast, around them. Some of these, too, should slope downwards.

6 Add short sprays of goldenrod and autumn leaves as fillers. Place the pedestal where it is not likely to be knocked over – a niche in a corner of a room is ideal. Remember to top up the container with water every day to keep the foam permanently moist.

THANKSGIVING FESTIVAL

A rustic basket filled with flowers, fruit, and foliage can take its place with pride at a harvest festival or at Thanksgiving, and looks equally good in the home, chapel, or church. Set in a window, shafts of golden autumn sunlight will flatter the russet colours of the plant materials, or use the composition to bring a warm glow to a shadowy corner.

1 The colour scheme of the arrangement makes the most of the tints and tones of the season, from the near-purple of the blackberry leaves and sedum to the pale pink of the climbing roses and hydrangeas; from the rosy blush of the pomegranates to the apricot hue of the spray chrysanthemums.

2 Place the waterproof liner in the basket. Place one whole block of foam in the dish and a half block in front of it. Secure each block in place by taping it from side to side with adhesive tape, over the foam and onto the container. Take another strip from front to back, over both of the foam blocks. Arrange some tall stems and branches at the back of the basket – fruiting crab apple looks magnificent – and short stems at the front on the other side.

3 Prepare the fruits that comprise the focal point of the arrangement. Pomegranates were used here but rosy apples, pears, or bunches of grapes could be used instead. Thread a stub wire through the fruit, close to the base. Twist the wire firmly and bend a hook in one end, to loop over the basket rim or into the foam.

4 Position the pomegranates or other fruit at the front of the arrangement, one dipping low over the basket rim, one resting on it, and the other close to the foam.

5 Cut the stems of the spray chrysanthemums to varying lengths and position them, tall, medium-height, and short, throughout the design.

6 Begin to fill in the arrangement with the thick, ruby-red heads of sedum, which make a striking contrast to the neighbouring chrysanthemums. Add accents of glossy red rosehips, and pale pink hydrangeas.

7 Position partly-opened roses next to the rosehips, and blackberry stems to border the design on one side. Complete the design by adding short sprays of glossy ivy; the green leaves make an interesting contrast to the autumn tints.

8 In this bountiful season, this fruit and flower arrangement looks at its best surrounded by more autumnal crops. A generous pile of apples and pears, marrows and pumpkins, and the pick of the falling leaves all add to the look of plenty.

GARLAND OF EVERGREENS

You Will Need

thick cord or rope • dry hay or sphagnum moss • green binding twine • scissors • evergreens such as blue pine • dried wheat • florists' scissors • secateurs (pruning shears) • gold spray paint • selection of pine and fir cones • hot glue • 7.5cm- (3in-) wide decorative ribbon • stub wire

The custom of bringing evergreens into our homes has its origins in the ancient world, when people believed them to have magical powers. A garland of evergreens, whether it is composed of blue pine, holly, or ivy, has the power to transform a corner of a room, a fireplace, or an arch and make it a decorative focal point at Christmastime.

1 This simple garland is composed of blue pine. Other materials could include Norwegian pine – the lower branches cut from the Christmas tree, perhaps – juniper, cypress, or many other evergreen species.

2 Measure the area where the garland is to hang, allowing for gentle curves and drapes and cut the rope to the required length. Tie the twine at one end of the rope. Take handfuls of hay or moss, wrap the material around the rope and bind it by taking the twine around it. Continue until the length, or lengths of rope are completely concealed beneath the natural material.

3 Cut the evergreen in short lengths and sprays. Place the first one over the hay-covered rope and bind it in place with the twine. Bind on more sprays, each one covering the stem end of the one before.

4 Gather the wheat in bunches of about six or seven heads and cut the stems to a total length of about 17.5cm (7in). Bind the stems with green twine. Place the bunches of wheat well apart on a newspaper and spray the heads with gold paint. Turn them over and spray them on the other side. Leave the paint to dry. Bind bunches of gilded wheat with the evergreens along the garland, first on one side and then the other.

5 When the length of the garland is completed, attach the cones. Drizzle spots of hot glue onto the pine at intervals and press on a cone. For the best appearance, alternate cones with long and rounded shapes.

6 Hang the garland in position and adjust it so that the evergreens, and not the hay-covered rope, are forward looking. Tie the ribbon into a bow, neaten the ends by cutting them at a slant, and thread the stub wire through the loop at the back. Attach the bow to the garland.

CHRISTMAS CHEER

You Will Need

*large flat plate; the one used here is
30cm (12in) diameter ● 2 plastic
prongs ● florists' adhesive clay
● scissors ● absorbent stem-holding
foam, soaked in water ● fruits,
nuts, and berries such as pineapple,
pomegranates, satsumas, lychees,
pecans, and iris seeds ● flowers
such as carnations, roses, and
spray chrysanthemums ● evergreens
such as ivy, yew, mahonia,
eucalyptus, and cypress ● florists'
scissors ● secateurs (pruning shears)*

Rose-coloured fruits and glossy nuts; gilded evergreens and glowing berries; coral carnations and vibrant roses – the materials bring together the natural gifts of the season in this outstanding Christmas decoration to display on a sideboard or side table, or as the centre of attraction on a buffet table.

1 The deep coral shades of the pomegranate and the iris seeds provided the colour cue for this arrangement; the principal flowers – the carnations and roses – were chosen to fit in with the scheme.

2 Make sure the plate is absolutely dry. Cut two short strips of adhesive clay and press one onto the underside of each of the plastic prongs. Press these onto the plate, one just behind the central point and one in front of it and to the right. Push blocks of soaked foam onto the prongs. Begin the arrangement by positioning a selection of evergreens to outline the height on one side and the depth of the design on the other.

3 Put the pineapple in place at the front of the plate. As it leans against the larger block of foam it should not need fixing into place. Position the carnations and roses through the design with the taller stems at the back. Note that several of the flowers face outwards from the sides of the design.

4 Position stems of spray chrysanthemums behind the other flowers where they will be seen as fillers rather than feature flowers. Arrange the iris berries on tall, medium, and short stems to distribute their contrasting texture throughout the design. Arrange trails of ivy low at the front.

5 Using hot glue, or quick-setting clear glue, stick several lychees together in a deep cluster. Thread a stub wire through a gap between the fruits, position them close to the pineapple and push the wire into the foam. Glue a cluster of pecans and position in a similar way, on the opposite side. Thread a stub wire through the back of a satsuma, twist the two ends and push the wire into the foam above the cluster of lychees. Tuck a pomegranate under the cascade of fruits and another (not illustrated) behind the iris stems on the other side.

6 Complete the design by adding more sprays of evergreens including, perhaps, trails of ivy sprayed with gold paint. Cover all traces of foam at the back of the arrangement with sprays of cypress and ivy. Arrange piles of fruit close to the design to complete the effect.

KISSING RING

You Will Need

stem wreath form; the one used here is 30cm (12in) diameter • wheat and linseed (flaxseed) seedheads • artificial Christmas roses • florists' scissors • gold spray paint • evergreens such as cypress, ivy, mistletoe, and eucalyptus • secateurs (pruning shears) • roll of florists' silver wire • stub wires • wire cutters • 7.5cm- (3in-) wide decorative ribbon

A bundle of wispy evergreens, clusters of gilded seedheads, a few sprigs of mistletoe, and two glittering bows make this the prettiest yuletide wreath ever. Hang it as a sign of welcome on the front door, on an internal wall or door or – a romantic notion – over a bed.

1 The wreath is designed to have an informal and slightly wayward look, so it is a good idea to avoid the darkest and heaviest of evergreens. Here, short sprays – hedge clippings – of lime-green cypress, slender trails of small-leafed ivy, eucalyptus, and mistletoe were used.

2 Cover the work surface with newspaper or scrap paper and spread out the wheat and linseed (flaxseed) seedheads, the artificial flowers, and any evergreens to be sprayed with gold paint. The degree of gilding in the design is a matter of personal preference. Here, a few of the ivy and eucalyptus stems were spatter-sprayed, but the leaves were not covered completely. Spray the materials on one side, then turn over and spray on the other. Leave to dry.

3 Gather the wheat into bunches of four or five stalks and bind them with silver wire. Gather the linseed (flaxseed) into bunches of uneven lengths – this gives the wispy look to the finished outline which is a feature of the design. Cut the evergreens into short lengths.

4 Cut several stub wires in half and bend them over to make U-shaped staples. Place a bunch of evergreens over the stem ring, loop a 'staple' over the stalks and press the wire ends into the wreath base.

5 Take a bunch of wheat and a piece of mistletoe, place so the heads cover the evergreen stems and staple in place. Continue adding evergreens and the other materials all around the ring, the heads of one cluster or bunch covering the stalks of the previous one.

6 Position the sprayed artificial flowers around the ring in an asymmetrical way. Wire stems can be pushed horizontally through the evergreens and into the wreath base. Tie two bows with the ribbon and neaten the ends by cutting them at a slant. Push half a stub wire through the loop at the back of each bow and insert into the wreath form.

7 Hang the wreath where it will catch flattering shafts of light to emphasize the gilding. To give your Christmas decorations a coordinated look, you could compose a smaller version of the wreath for a table decoration.

CHRISTMAS GREETINGS

You Will Need

selection of evergreens such as blue pine, ivy, cypress, and yew • dried grasses • wheat • gold spray paint • roll of florists' silver wire • 4cm- (1½in-) wide decorative ribbon

Welcome callers with a simple evergreen door posy, or make several to decorate the house during the festive season.

1 Cover the work surface with newspaper and spray a few heads of wheat and some trails of ivy with gold paint. Turn the materials over and spray them on the other side. Leave them to dry. Gather the wheat in a bunch of uneven lengths and bind the stems with silver wire. Tie the grass stems into a bunch and wire them.

2 Place the largest component, the blue pine, on the table and arrange the other materials over it. Rearrange them until they form a pleasing shape. Bind all the stems together with silver wire. Tie the ribbon around the stems, tie into a bow and trim the ends by cutting at a slant.

TARTAN TRIO

Give plain white candles a festive look with bright trimmings of evergreens, berries, and ribbons. You can use them to decorate a window, a mantelpiece, or the dining table.

1 Cut short lengths of mixed evergreens and seedheads. Place a few stems against a candle and bind in place with silver wire. Add more stems, and bind in place around the candle until it is decorated with a ring of evergreens. Secure the binding wire. Hook the wires of the berry decorations over the silver wire. Tie a ribbon around the candle to conceal the wire, tie it in a bow and trim the ends.

2 Display the candles among cuttings of evergreens. Do not leave lighted candles unattended.

WEDDING CELEBRATION

You Will Need

*pedestal-type fruit bowl or container
• piece of plastic-covered wire
mesh netting • narrow florists'
adhesive tape • scissors • selection
of flowers such as lilies, roses,
Singapore orchids, mimosa, spray
chrysanthemums, and
chincherinchee • sprays of
variegated foliage • florists' scissors*

Triumphant white lilies, delicate cream roses, exotic Singapore orchids, palest yellow mimosa – they all combine in an arrangement to capture the attention of the most starry-eyed bride. When the toasts are proposed, glasses are sure to be raised to the 'friend who did the flowers'.

1 Make your choice of flowers to complement the colour scheme chosen by the bride. This selection, in white, cream, and yellow, was chosen to add a hint of warmth to a winter-white scheme. Use a piece of wire mesh netting wide enough to fill the bowl. Hold it firmly in place with two criss-crossing strips of adhesive tape threaded through the wires, and short lengths looped around the wire and stuck onto the container at intervals.

2 Arrange the mimosa sprays to fan out from all sides of the bowl. When mimosa is not in season, or if the yellow flowers do not suit the colour scheme, slender sprays of foliage can be used instead. Arrange short stems of variegated foliage all around the rim of the container.

3 Arrange the lilies at two levels, with the fully-opened flowers facing the front of the design. Turn the container around and arrange more lilies in a similar way on the other side. The arrangement must be equally attractive when viewed from all sides.

4 Arrange a cluster of roses at the heart of the design, where the soft pale cream petals will emphasize the pure whiteness of the lilies. Arrange more roses in a similar position on the reverse of the bowl, then position the orchids to form a point in the centre. Position a few stems of chincherinchee on either side of the orchids.

5 Flatter the exotic flowers still further by arranging the simple daisy shapes of spray chrysanthemums in clusters between them. Spray the flowers with a fine mist of cool water, and keep the arrangement in a cool, shady place until the festivities begin.

GOING FOR GOLD

When there's a 50th wedding anniversary to celebrate; someone you know has just been awarded a gold medal or gold watch; or you just want to put on a glittering party – go for gold. Our arrangement features a plain glass vase which has been dazzlingly transformed for the occasion with a handful of chocolate wrappers and a few dabs of glue. It's an idea you can adapt to create a variety of kaleidoscopic effects, using multi-coloured wrappers or metallic papers in a random patchwork.

1 Cut short stems of wheat and linseed (flaxseed), group them into bunches and bind the stems with silver wire or twine. Cover a surface with newspaper and spray the wheat, linseed (flaxseed), and hydrangea with gold paint. Leave the materials to dry. The gold chocolate wrappings are stuck patchwork-fashion to the inside of the vase. A long-handled paintbrush is useful to manoeuvre and press them into place.

2 Shape the stem-holding foam to fit the plastic container by pressing the holder over the unsoaked block. Withdraw the container and cut around the imprint with a sharp knife. Soak the now circular piece of foam in water until it is saturated.

3 Cut two or three strips of adhesive clay, and press to the underside of the plastic holder. Press the holder onto the neck of the vase. Insert the soaked foam. (This vase had a raised rim which fitted closely around the plastic container, so it was not necessary to secure it further by taping over the foam with florists' adhesive tape). Create the outline of the arrangement with stems of eucalyptus, making a lop-sided triangle. Place other stems, and some sprays of flowering shrub, at the centre of the design.

4 Arrange the carnations to follow the overall outline of the design, then position the bunches of wheat and linseed (flaxseed) to fill the gaps. If the wheat stalks are too supple to push into the foam, it may be necessary to wrap a stub wire around the bunch and push one extended end into it.

5 Arrange the spray chrysanthemums around the design. If some of the sprays seem too dense, cut off one or two of the flowers and position the short stems at the front, where they will help to conceal the foam. Place the gold-sprayed hydrangea head in the centre, as a secondary and glittering focal point.

6 Position the spray carnations and cut off any small buds that interfere with the flow of the stems. Cut short sprays of gypsophila and place them around the base of the arrangement, where they will separate the golden-coloured flowers and create light spots. Tie a gold ribbon around the neck of the vase if desired.

PARTY PIECE

Flowers arranged for a buffet party or a special family celebration can use artistic licence in the matter of colour, break some of the rules, and earn nothing but praise. This party piece proves that you can blend red, blue, orange, mauve, yellow, and green – all the colours of the rainbow – in an arrangement that will command attention across a crowded room.

1 This is an occasion when you can give way to the temptation to choose several bunches of flowers of different types, colours, shapes, and sizes; when it is more important to match the mood of the occasion than the surrounding furnishings. Cut all the stem ends at a sharp angle, to facilitate the intake of water, and give the flowers a long drink in cool water before arranging them.

3 Arrange the Peruvian lilies – here deep coral, peach, and cream colours were used – to follow the outline of the foliage. Cut some of the individual flowers on short stems and position them close to the foam.

2 Stick a piece of adhesive clay to the underside of the plastic prong – some arrangers call it a 'frog's leg' – and press onto the container slightly behind the centre point. Press the soaked foam onto the spikes of the prong. Arrange the various types of foliage to make a fan shape across the centre of the arrangement, and to cascade down over the rim of the container at the front and sides.

4 Arrange the orchids in a triangular shape throughout the design, the tallest stem upright in the centre and progressively shorter stems slanted outwards at the front. If cutting the stems short involves cutting off some of the lower florets, position these as attractive 'fillers' close to the foam.

5 Arrange the irises to make a patch of contrasting colour – the only blue in the design – at the back. Cut the stems at a sharply slanting angle. The lower part of the stem and the sword-like leaves can be used at the reverse of the arrangement. Turn the container around and fill in the back of the design with sprays of foliage and a selection of flowers to give the arrangement depth and perspective.

6 Complete the arrangement by adding the softening influence – as far as the shape is concerned – of the roses and carnations, which contrast well with the principally trumpet- and star-like shapes of the other flowers. Add more foliage sprays to fill in any gaps, and check that the design looks equally good from either side.

A NOTE OF FORMALITY

When you are giving a formal dinner party – it may be for 'elder statesmen' in the family, business associates, or in celebration of an anniversary – the flower arrangements should set the tone of the occasion. This arrangement for the dining table is an all-round design in a silver-coloured urn, a profusion of flowers and foliage in white, cream, and silvery green.

1 Whether the dining table is set with crisp white linen or presents a highly polished surface; whether the china is ornately patterned or plain white – flowers in white, cream, and the palest of yellow compose a flatteringly pretty accessory.

2 Begin by building up the foundation of the design, the background of the mimosa, foliage, and hydrangea heads against which the more showy plant materials are seen. Arrange the mimosa sprays to form a fan shape on one side, tuck short clusters of hydrangea over the rim of the container, and position soft, silver-grey foliage such as ballota midway between them. Repeat the shape, if not the detail, on the other side.

3 Position the orchids to emphasize the central height, and fill in the middle ground with chincherinchee, Peruvian lilies, spray chrysanthemums, and roses.

4 Turn the container around and repeat the flower sequence on the other side, cutting the stems to achieve height balance.

5 Add short sprays of foliage to separate the flowers, so that each type can be seen to advantage. Turn the container around and check that the reverse is equally attractive. Add more flowers or foliage to correct any visual deficiencies.

BRIDESMAID'S HEADDRESS

You Will Need

stub wires • roll of florists' silver wire • white gutta percha (floral) tape • scissors • selection of flowers such as spray chrysanthemums, delphiniums, and roses • florists' scissors • 2.5cm- (1in-) wide patterned ribbon

A pretty circlet to be worn by a bridesmaid or a young bride at a summer wedding. The colours, a striking blend of apricot, cream, and blue, were chosen to complement the pale peach dresses of the young attendants in a country church.

1 To give the headdress more variety of colour, slender stems of dark blue larkspur and delphinium were blended with large florets, in a paler tint, cut from long spires of a similar plant. This also has the advantage of including flowers from a favourite garden without visibly denuding it.

2 You can make the base of the headdress from a piece of thick wire bound into a circle or, as was done here, use two stub wires twisted together to form a hoop. In either case, bind the wire with gutta percha (floral) tape, which is self-adhesive, taking it around the wire so that each strip overlaps the previous one.

3 Cut the flower stems to a length of about 4cm (1½in). Gather them into clusters of one or two spray chrysanthemums, a short spray of larkspur, and a delphinium floret. Bind the stems with a few twists of silver wire, and bind the cluster to the circle with the wire. Wire on a rose, more flower clusters, another rose and so on, until the floral circle is complete.

4 Tie the ribbon into a bow with long, trailing ends. Neaten the ends by cutting them at a slant. Thread the silver wire through the back of the ribbon loop and bind the bow to the headdress. Spray the flowers with a fine mist of cool water, and keep the decoration in a cool place – even in the refrigerator – until moments before setting off for the ceremony.

5 If the headdress is to be carried on a journey, wrap it carefully, perhaps in tissue paper in a box. Do not leave it in the full glare of the sun on the back seat of a car. A corsage, to be worn by a principal wedding guest, may be composed of similar flowers.

TABLE GARLAND

A garland is a lovely way to decorate a wedding or christening reception, a birthday, or other celebration. The garland, composed of long leafy stems, can be made to loop across the front of the buffet table, to encircle the rim of a table displaying the cake, or to drape on all four sides of a free-standing table.

1 Smilax, with its pliable stem and mass of bright green leaves forms a natural garland, and makes an attractive instant decoration, even without the addition of flowers. It is usually sold to order in bundles of five stems. Keep the stem ends in water until just before you assemble the garland, and the foliage should stay fresh for several days.

2 It saves time just before the event if the posies are made up in advance. Choose materials which will contrast well with the bright but delicate foliage of the garland. Cut the flower stems short, using five or six pieces of gypsophila, two small snippings of mimosa, and one or two spray chrysanthemums, according to their size. Gather the stems together and bind them with silver roll wire.

3 The posies can be spaced as close together or as wide apart as desired. As a general rule, the smaller the table the smaller the gap should be between the flowers.

Once the posies are assembled they can be placed in a shallow bowl of water before being attached to the garland.

4 Measure the length of garland needed for the side drapes and mark the centre. With the stems of the first posy towards the end of one of the lengths of foliage, bind the posy to the main stem with roll wire. Bind on more posies in the same way, reversing the direction of the stems when you reach the centre of the draped garland. Repeat the decoration with the remaining lengths of garland, but without reversing the direction of the flowers of the side trails.

5 Pin the garland to the cloth, adjusting the fall of the drape so that it is equal on all sides, and pin on the side trails. Check that the garland hangs well. Sometimes the weight of the posies will cause it to twist, with the flowers facing inwards. If this happens, pin the garland to the cloth at intervals. Pin ribbon or bows to the corners and the centre of the drapes.

WEDDING DECORATION

Hanging decorations in a church or chapel complement the larger arrangements, the pedestal and windowsill designs, and further enhance the setting for a wedding or baptism. Such decorations may hang on the ends of pews, or on pillars, posts, and altar screens.

1 Before planning the wall decorations, take note of the background colour, whether it is dark oak or light pine, a relatively plain surface or a heavily-grained wood that is seen as a distinct pattern. Then choose the flower and foliage colours accordingly. If, for example, the theme of the wedding calls for flowers in pale colours, and the background wood is honey-coloured pine, give the design a clear, if wayward outline with dark foliage, and include some darker flowers to avoid a faded look. If making more than one decoration, divide the flowers and foliage into groups so that each matches the other.

2 Press a slice cut from a block of soaked foam into the plastic holder. Holding the container vertically, check that the foam is held firmly in place; it should be, because such holders are purpose-made for the size of the foam block. If it does not seem secure, tape the foam in place with two strips of florists' adhesive tape. Arrange long stems of slender foliage at the top and bottom of the holder and shorter sprays in the centre.

3 Cut short a carnation stem and position it just above the centre of the foam. Arrange the irises above and below it. Cut individual Peruvian lily flowers and arrange them to form the background of the design.

4 Arrange short sprays of foliage and flowering shrub to isolate some of the flowers and avoid a crowded look.

5 Extend the outline of the design with spray carnations. Cut the narrow ribbon into three lengths, double each one, and tie into a bow. Thread half a stub wire through the back of the loop, twist the ends, and press into the foam. Fold two or three lengths of wide ribbon in half, twist half a stub wire around the centre, twist the ends, and push them into the foam at the base of the decoration. Hang the decoration by threading a wire or length of twine through the hole in the handle. Spray the flowers with a fine mist of cool water, and keep them in a cool, shady place until needed.

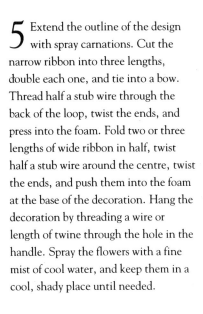

FIT FOR A BRIDE

You Will Need

stub wires • wire cutters • roll of florists' silver wire • white gutta percha (floral) tape • scissors • selection of flowers such as Singapore orchids, Peruvian lilies, chincherinchee, irises, narcissus, mimosa, and freesias • florists' scissors • 4cm- (1½in-) wide satin ribbon • selection of foliage such as ballota and pampas grass

For a close friend or a relative of the bride it is both a pleasure and a privilege to compose the wedding bouquet. Confirm her preference for flower types and colours, then follow our easy step-by-step instructions for a bouquet fit for the most discerning bride.

1 Design the bride's bouquet to feature the flowers and colours that will set the scene for the ceremony and the reception and complement the colours she and her attendants will wear. If the bride's dress is in off-white or cream, avoid using pure-white flowers which would be unflattering to the fabric. Give all the flowers a long drink of cool water in a shady place before composing the bouquet.

2 It is essential to wire flowers for a bouquet of this kind, otherwise the bundle of stems forming the handle would both look and feel clumsy. Cut short the flower stems and push a stub wire into the ends. Bind over the join and down along the wire with overlapping gutta percha (floral) tape.

3 Gather together all the flowers that will form the centre of the bouquet – orchids, Peruvian lilies, freesias, and a rose – and bind the false wire stems with silver wire.

4 Hold the core of the bouquet in one hand and arrange slender stems of foliage to cascade over the flowers. Arrange a second layer of flowers around the front and sides of the central ones and bind all the stems and false stems with silver wire.

5 Arrange a third layer of flowers around the front and sides of the bouquet, bind the stems with silver wire, and add a few feature flowers close to the grip. Roses and short sprays of mimosa look attractive in this position. Bind the stems again with silver wire, and then with the satin ribbon, tying it just under the lowest of the flowers. Tie the ribbon in a bow and leave long, trailing ends. Spray the flowers with a fine mist of cool water, and keep in a cool place – even the refrigerator – until the ceremony is imminent.

BRIDAL POSY

Delicate and pretty summer flowers are arranged in colourful rings for a bridesmaid's posy that owes more than a little to Victorian styles. It is a design that would find favour with young brides, too, and is traditional enough to fulfil the requirement for 'something old' while comprising richly-coloured delphinium to provide 'something blue'.

1 If desired, the flower stems may be cut short, mounted on wires and bound with gutta percha (floral) tape before creating the bridal posy. In this design, which is seen as an informal posy and not a bouquet, the flowers are simply gathered together as a bunch. Give the flowers and foliage a long drink in cool water in a shady place before arranging them, since they will have no moisture source.

2 Gather the delphinium stems into a bunch and bind – not too tightly – with silver wire. Cut off any leaves that look out of place and obscure the flowers.

3 Holding the delphinium bunch in one hand, arrange first the freesias and then the spray carnations in graded layers around them. Rearrange the stems until the flower heads appear in neat rings. Bind the stems loosely with silver wire.

4 Arrange the ring of roses above the delphinium, where the delicate round flowers will contrast prettily with the dark spires. Arrange a few dainty sprays of foliage such as eucalyptus among the flowers, and position a rose beneath the ring of spray carnations. Rearrange the stems until the flowers rest in a pleasing sequence, then bind the stems with silver wire. If you make the posy a day before the wedding, leave it in water overnight before covering the stems with ribbon.

5 Wrap one end of the ribbon around the stems immediately beneath the rose and make a knot to secure it. Bind the stems with the ribbon and finish with a bow. Spray the flowers with a fine mist of cool water, avoiding the ribbon, and keep the posy in a cool place, perhaps in the refrigerator, until it is needed.

PASTEL TINTS

A circlet of summer's palest and prettiest flowers – sweet peas, roses, carnations, and more – makes a delightful decoration for a garden party or an outdoor reception. To set the scene for a country wedding you could make these rings to match the bridal headdresses.

1 Short sprays and snippings of flowers can be used in this design, perhaps stems left over after composing larger arrangements for the occasion. Arrange a ring of ivy leaves around the inside and outside of the ring form to frame the flowers. Cut each sweet pea flower on a short stem and arrange them at intervals around the ring.

2 Complete the ring of sweet peas and arrange more ivy leaves between the flowers, to give the design a natural and countrified look.

3 Cut individual flowers of roses, Peruvian lilies and spray carnations and arrange them between the sweet peas. Some of the flowers should be placed around the inside and outside rims of the ring form. Cut short sprays of gypsophila and arrange them all around the ring. These diminutive white flowers have a soft veil-like effect and give the design a pretty look of informality.

4 A floral circlet can decorate a table top, a low shelf – where it may be seen against a stretch of green lawn – or a buffet table, where it would make an unusual centre-piece.

DRIED FLOWERS AND FLOWERCRAFT

~

Preserving flowers, foliage, seedheads, and bracts is a delightfully simple yet infinitely satisfying pastime, and one which enables you to accumulate a collection of colourful and contrasting plant materials throughout the year. You can preserve materials from the garden or the countryside, dry flowers from a romantic gift or a wedding bouquet, or buy them from the ever-increasing variety available from florists.

We explain the preserving techniques in detail and then, in a series of step-by-step arrangements, show you how to enjoy your everlasting harvest in designs to decorate every room in the home and enhance every occasion.

A shallow bowl of paper-dry roses and carnations glowing in the candlelight; a profusion of flowers from all seasons classically arranged in a gilded urn; a pretty bridal bouquet of purple orchids and cream strawflowers that will become a treasured memento; a bowl lined with fragrant potpourri and luxuriant with flowers dried from the garden; a highly textured ring of pressed autumn leaves in deep, rich browns; and a charming gift basket composed of realistic fabric flowers: the art of decorating with preserved and man-made plant materials can transform every room in the house. With flowers, leaves, seedheads, and bracts that you have preserved yourself or bought from a shop, you can compose colourful and contrasting arrangements to give pleasure for months to come.

Colour, texture, and the infinite variety of combinations are the exciting keynotes of preserved materials. Brilliant pink peonies from a summer border; delphinium spires in deepest blue; statice and strawflowers in colours spanning the rainbow; bright scarlet iris seedpods, muted poppy and rue pods and old man's beard, offering woody and feathery textures. Using the variety of materials available, your designs can be as vibrant and colourful or as subtle and restrained as you like.

Collecting and preserving plant materials is a fulfilling and fascinating pastime you can enjoy throughout the year. If you have access to a garden, you can gather a few flowers from the borders as each season comes around, and preserve them using the simple methods described in the following pages. In summer you can cut branches of deciduous leaves and, later, bracts and berries to preserve, supple and glowing bright, in a solution of glycerin. As autumn approaches, you can cut seedheads and hang them to dry, or even dye them in natural-looking or more adventurous shades.

A walk in the woods becomes a treasure hunt for cones, interesting twigs, fallen leaves, pieces of gnarled wood, nuts, and acorns. A country walk may yield by the roadside a patch of wild oats, scattered wheat, interesting grasses, and other seedheads, partly dried on the plants and requiring only a few days in a warm, dry atmosphere to become practically everlasting. Even a walk on the beach will provide material. Pieces of sea-bleached driftwood make wonderful backdrops for dried-flower designs. Shells, if large enough, make luxurious-looking containers for dried flowers, and add a welcome sparkle to the design; and if small, they make light-catching and reflective accessories to a floral group. Coloured pebbles are a natural and attractive stem-holding material, while windswept stems of sea lavender, reeds, and rushes are all useful, versatile, and neutral filler materials.

A colourful container fitted with crumpled wire mesh netting holds the key to an arrangement of scarlet and orange berries – iris and pyracantha (firethorn) respectively – dried grasses and exotic seedheads. Many of these, bought without stems, are mounted on stub wires which are concealed among the surrounding materials. **Left**

Dried plant materials from the garden and wayside mingle in a casual grouping designed for the kitchen or dining room. The rugged basket is woven from bleached willow. **Opposite**

Florists' shops, department stores, boutiques, and even antique shops have a vast range of dried and preserved flowers and leaves for sale. Ceilings hanging with a floral arbour of dried flowers; buckets of preserved leaves; baskets and packets of exotic seedheads, many imported and perhaps unfamiliar – retail shops offer such variety and temptation, and are a useful source of materials for a growing collection. You could buy a bunch of rich pink dried rosebuds and dark blue larkspur and, with a few clippings of dried foliage and bracts, create a pretty countrified arrangement in an old teapot. The design illustrated below had matching afore-thought. The teapot and jug, both flea market bargains, are spatter-painted in pink and blue, the tiny speckled pattern a perfect foil for the contrasting round and spire shapes.

You could buy an assortment of dried seedheads, some like ornately carved ornaments, and mount them on stub-wire stems (many are sold stemless), then blend them with reds and greens from your collection. There might be lotus flower seedheads, trumpet-shaped and peppered with holes; luffa (loofah) seedpods with their chestnut-brown colouring and high-ridged texture; protea flowers, a striking combination of wood-brown and silver sold at various stages of development; jhuta pods like wide-open sculpted flowers; and plumosum heads with their wayward spiky appearance. Take any two or three of these plant types, arrange them with feathery and frondy

materials – the very antithesis of their harsh outlines – and you have created a plant sculpture. The 'Eastern Riches' project in which the materials are arranged in a yogurt pot – you could equally use a wide-necked jug – shows only one of the effects that can be achieved.

HARVESTING PLANT MATERIALS

It can be immensely satisfying to gather plant materials from a garden or in the wild, knowing that by preserving them you can prolong or even enhance their decorative life. Many flowers and some leaves can be preserved by air-drying – often no more than being hung in bunches in a warm, airy room – and a wide range of others can be dried in a desiccant. Leaves gathered when the sap is still rising in the plant, as well as some bracts, can be preserved, glowing and supple, in a solution of water and glycerin, and may take on shades and tints more attractive even than those of autumn.

Before launching into the countryside with a pair of secateurs or pruning shears, take note that stringent restrictions apply to the cutting of wild plants. These limitations vary from country to country and state to state, according to the local abundance or scarcity of plant types; what is a rampant weed in one area may be a protected species in another. Be sure you know the rules before cutting even one stem.

An old teapot and jug – unremarkable in their original state – were spatter-painted in colours which link the dried flowers to the Indian rug in the background. The delphinium stems are arranged with a curve to the right, towards the jug which, with its trio of exotic seedheads, becomes an important accessory in this still-life group. **Right**

Gather these materials – lavender, rosebuds, wheat, and grasses – at the height of summer, dry them in a warm, dry atmosphere, and enjoy the fragrant arrangement for months to come. **Left**

A dried-flower tree makes an attractive table or windowsill decoration that is both easy to make and long lasting. This one, composed on a dry foam sphere on a knobbly twig, is studded with white statice, lavender, and a variety of seedheads. **Below**

FLOWERS

Plant material for drying should, ideally, be harvested when it is completely free of extraneous moisture. If you have to gather flowers when they are wet, toss them gently on blotting paper to remove surface water, and stand the stems in a container of water in a warm, dry room until the petals are thoroughly dry. Do not be tempted to start one of the drying processes while the flowers are still damp. The development of mould will rapidly gain ground on the drying technique – a recipe for disappointment.

The time of day is also a contributory factor to successful drying. It is best to gather the flowers for drying before or after the sun is at its highest; it does not matter about seedheads. At high noon the plant is at its most vulnerable, and more inclined to wilt than respond to the drying treatment.

Flowers to be dried by one of the free-circulation-of-air techniques include many of those which may be described as multi-floral stems – clarkia, delphinium, heather, larkspur, and mimosa, among others – and those composed of a mass of florets – achillea (yarrow), golden-rod, and lady's mantle are examples. Flowers of this type are best harvested at the mid-way stage of their development. In the case of delphinium, this means when some of the lowest florets are fully opened, the ones above them are just beginning to unfurl, and the top-most buds are still tightly closed.

Other flowers that dry successfully in warm air are those composed of a mass of petals, such as cornflowers, love-in-a-mist, and pot marigolds. These should be harvested just before they are fully opened. All everlastings, including statice and strawflowers, are also well suited to

The gourds placed beside the dried flower and seed arrangement, echoing the raised pattern on the jug, are seen as complementary accessories. The flowers and seedheads, in a low colour key, include lady's mantle, strawflowers, statice, linseed (flaxseed), wheat, and bells of Ireland. **Left**

A glorious array of dried flowers forms the prettiest of veils for a north-facing bedroom window. The blue and white jug is fitted with crumpled wire mesh netting to secure the profusion of delphinium, rosebuds, sea lavender, and strawflowers. **Opposite**

this drying technique. If the weather is favourable, these flowers may be left on the plant until they are crackle-dry, but in unsettled conditions, when storms or strong gales are forecast, it is best to gather them on a dry day and hang them in bunches indoors to complete the drying process that is part of their natural cycle.

Desiccant drying opens up opportunities to preserve jewel-bright anemones, golden narcissus, and fragrant stems of lily-of-the-valley, as well as camellias, orchids, roses, and many other species. These may be harvested at any stage of their cycle, from tiny bud to full-blown bloom. In terms of design versatility, it can be rewarding to gather a few flowers at a time, and preserve them at the various stages of their development. In that way, you can capture the natural progression of each flower, and enjoy the variety of shape and colour in arrangements that will be a reminder of a continuing harvest.

Alternatively, you can cut flowers at an early stage and arrange them, fresh, just the way they are. Then, when they are just at their peak, you can preserve them in desiccant. This approach allows you to enjoy the beauty of fresh flowers before you preserve them, which is particularly welcome when you have been given a special token of flowers. Keep a watchful eye on them and preserve the flowers for all time.

SEEDHEADS

Harvesting seedheads for drying offers further rich pickings in terms of shape and texture, as many of the photographs here show. You might like to arrange a cluster of poppy seedheads in a winter garden composition in a basket, their clearly defined, urn-like shapes making a dramatic silhouette. You might choose to arrange a handful of linseed (flaxseed) heads, the tiny ball-like

The air-drying process has long-term decorative potential. Hanging in bunches and standing upright in containers, the flowers and seedheads can decorate the corner of a room, or compose a still-life group.
Right

shapes an attractive foil to spiky ears of wheat and petal-packed peonies in a design with more than a hint of the 1930s. Or in a different mood, you might decide to combine fluffy heads of hare's-tail grass, wheat ears, lavender seedheads, and silvery honesty 'moons' with dried ruby-red roses as a romantic decoration for a heart-shaped vine wreath form.

Seedhead gathering is a less exacting science than harvesting flowers, though it is desirable to leave the seed carriers on wild plants until the seeds have scattered and the following year's crop is assured. Moisture is the only threat, so gather the stems when they are dry, or, if this is not possible, toss them on absorbent paper and hang or stand them loosely in bunches in a dry place. Do not allow damp seedheads to jostle together. When air cannot circulate freely between plant materials trouble occurs in the form of bacterial growth.

FOLIAGE

Preserved leaves are an invaluable component in dried-flower compositions of all kinds. Long foliage sprays such as eucalyptus can be used to 'sketch in' the outline of arrangements before the flowers are positioned, and small sprays of dried leaves arranged among dried rosebuds and carnations separate the flowers, allowing each to be seen in clear outline. Foliage is also ideal for concealing the holding materials of a design. It is well worthwhile building up a collection of preserved leaves to supplement and complement your dried flowers and seedheads.

A few types of foliage can be preserved by the air-drying method, including sage, santolina, lavender, lady's mantle, and hops. Many more can be dried in a desiccant, and both evergreens and deciduous leaves can be preserved in glycerin. For the most satisfactory results, it is best to gather deciduous leaves once they have fully matured on the tree or shrub, and while the sap is still rising. Beautiful as they are in their soft-green immaturity, young leaves do not take well to the preserving processes,

and will wilt under the strain. Evergreens have a longer harvest potential, but even those should not be cut when they are showing young green shoots.

AIR-DRYING PLANT MATERIALS

The simplest and most widely used method of preserving plant materials is by air-drying, which may mean no more than leaving them in a suitable room where warm, dry air can circulate freely around them. This process is not an exact science and the actual temperature is not critical, though it should not fall below 10°C (50°F.) More important is the humidity: a damp, steamy atmosphere where the windows are streaming with condensation is definitely not one in which to dry flowers. In conditions like this, the materials will absorb moisture more quickly than they shed it. This rules out, as the drying room, some kitchens, bathrooms, and utility rooms, and many garden sheds or garages. However, living rooms and bedrooms can be used successfully, and bunches of flowers hanging from the ceiling, on a pole across a room corner, on an airing rack, or on coathangers on a wall can be a positive decorative feature.

Some plant types, mostly those with a heavy head-to-stem ratio, give the best results when dried upright, the stems loosely held in tall containers and the heads fanning out wide and away from each other to ensure the free circulation of air. Materials in this category include umbrella-shaped flowers and seedheads, also known as umbellifers, such as achillea (yarrow), fennel, caraway, and onion seedheads; others in that family include pampas grass, globe artichokes, linseed (flaxseed), and corn cobs (Indian corn).

Other flowers and foliage may be dried horizontally, spread out on racks or shelves covered with absorbent paper. Dock and sorrel seedheads, grasses, and lavender are among the plant types that respond well to this method, but they will do so only if they are first arranged in a single layer and then turned at frequent intervals. Change the paper if it becomes the slightest bit damp.

Some plant materials may be air-dried, though it seems a contradiction in terms, with their stems standing in a little water, no more than 4–5 cm (1½–2in). The principle is that as the stems gradually absorb the water it evaporates and eventually, over a week or ten days, the plant material dries more or less naturally. Flowers and bracts in this category include cornflowers, mimosa, gypsophila, pearl (pearly) everlasting, and hydrangea.

Many plant types can be dried by more than one method. It is often a matter of choice and convenience whether you hang flowers and seedheads in bunches, stand them in a container, or spread them out flat. To repeat, drying is not an exact science, and there is plenty of scope for choice and experimentation.

Whatever drying method you choose, the choice and preparation of plant materials is of paramount importance. It is simply not worth preserving bird-damaged sprays of foliage or flowers that are even slightly discoloured. Snip off any unsightly leaves – the largest ones of purple sage, for example, are prone to turn brittle and brown around the edges, and will never revive – and pull off any off-colour flower petals. It is often possible to rescue flowers, especially roses, which show only minimal damage to their petals.

In a few cases, leaves will air-dry almost as satisfactorily as the flowers on the same stems; roses are a good example. In others, the leaves become brittle and snap off, so it is best to remove them at the preparation stage. Chinese lanterns (winter cherry) are a case in point. While the seedpods, changing from pale green to brilliant orange, dry to perfection, the leaves fall to the ground. Strip off any leaves and florets that would be squashed and trapped under the string when they are tied in bunches. If the air cannot reach all of the plant material rot sets in and impairs the drying process.

Materials to be dried by hanging should be tied into small bunches, with large stems tied individually. Arrange candidates for upright or horizontal drying accordingly, and leave the materials in a warm, dry place for several days. After that, check every two or three days. When dry enough – when they feel crisp and papery – remove them from the extra warmth of an airing cupboard or boiler cupboard and store them at ordinary room temperature, but still in a dry atmosphere. You can store materials as you please and as you dry them. They make an attractive feature hanging in bunches or standing in containers, or they can be packed carefully in boxes until needed.

DRYING IN WATER

Hydrangea heads and gypsophila, so different in size, shape, and form, are two of the plant materials which can be air-dried with their stems standing in a little water.

*Give a hearth-side decoration
an airing when having drinks
or tea on the patio. The design
includes peonies and rosebuds,
sea lavender and strawflowers,
marjoram and carthamus.*
Opposite

*If a kitchen is well ventilated,
then air-drying or dried herbs
and flowers hanging in bunches
can be a homely and attractive
feature. They are also
conveniently on hand when
needed for cooking or
garnishing.* **Right**

DRYING IN DESICCANTS

When that time comes, you may have enough air-dried materials to compose a towering arrangement to stand in the hearth. There could be acanthus and achillea (yarrow) flowers, goldenrod and globe amaranth, tansy and timothy grass. On a smaller scale, you could bind dried flowers into a posy and hang on a chair back or bedpost: pretty, creamy-white feverfew combined with strawflowers and rosebuds, lady's mantle and lavender, all tied with trailing ribbons.

But as far as drying is concerned, this represents little more than the tip of the iceberg. By adding the technique of drying in desiccants you can extend your collection to include trumpet- and cone-shaped flowers, such as daffodils and freesia; composites like spray chrysanthemums, marguerites, and other daisy forms; open-faced flowers, such as pansies, anemones, and buttercups; high-density flowers like ranunculus, carnations, and many more.

If air-drying is seen as an almost natural technique, in which air alone draws out the plant moisture, then desiccant-drying may be thought of as the scientific approach. In this method, any one of a number of drying agents may be used to fill every cavity and crevice of the plant material, cover every part of every surface and, in so doing, support the flower and keep it perfectly in shape. That is why hollow and flat forms, which would collapse or wilt during the air-drying process, emerge from the desiccant having lost none of their original characteristics, and looking as fresh as ever. The 'Candle Glow' arrangement uses flowers dried in this way.

Your choice of desiccant may depend on the quantity and scale of the plant materials you intend to dry. But be warned: once you have experienced the thrill of gently scraping away the crystals or powder to discover the perfectly dried forms of, say, trumpet-shaped mallow flowers, purple-spotted foxgloves, and fully-opened roses you may never want to stop!

TYPES OF DESICCANT

The desiccant options available are alum powder (aluminum sulfate) and household borax, both of which may be bought in chemists (drugstores) and are suitable for small, delicate flower types; ground silica gel crystals, available in some chemists, florists' shops and camera retailers, and suitable for all the small-to-medium-sized flowers and above; corn meal, from grocers and supermarkets, for flowers of all sizes; and dry silver sand, recommended for drying large quantities of sizeable materials, such as dahlias and mophead chrysanthemums.

Silica gel crystals are available in two forms – standard white crystals, which look like colourless coffee sugar, and the colour-changing type that have a built-in moisture indicator. These crystals are bright blue when they are dry and ready to use, and turn white and then pink when they are damp. If bought in large crystal form silica gel is too heavy to be used successfully for drying flowers, and you have to grind it into fine crystals – not quite to a powder –

using a pestle and mortar, or an electric blender or food processor. If you do use an electric appliance, take it to an open window before removing the lid. A swirl of very fine dust, which looks like thick fog, will rush upwards as you do so. It can cause irritation to the throat and eyes, so keep the appliance well away from your face.

You may like to experiment by using a combination of two or more of the desiccants. Adding, say, one part silica gel crystals or dry silver sand to two or three parts alum or borax helps to overcome a problem commonly experienced when either of the powders is used alone: they both have tenacious sticking properties, and can be difficult to brush off dry and brittle petals. You may also like to weigh up the relative costs, though over the long term the difference becomes almost negligible since all the desic-

cants can be sieved to remove any scraps of petals or leaves that may have been displaced, spread on baking trays, and dried in an oven at low temperature. Put in the oven a tray of bright pink silica gel crystals that have drawn out the moisture from a box of carnations, leave it for half an hour or so, and retrieve sky-blue crystals ready for use. Allow the desiccants to cool, then store them in an airtight tin or jar. In this way, desiccants can be used almost indefinitely. Some flower-arranging enthusiasts of our acquaintance have just celebrated the 20th anniversary of a tin full of silica gel!

METHODS

The method is simple. Spread a thin layer of desiccant in a container, arrange the flowers and foliage sprays according to type, well spaced and with no two items touching, and cover them gently, gradually, and completely with desiccant until it forms a top layer about 1.5cm (½in) above the plant material.

The type of container you use depends on the speed of the drying method you choose. The traditional, slow way

A heart-shaped vine wreath form decorated with dried flowers would make a delightfully romantic Valentine or birthday gift. The posies of roses, sea lavender, honesty,

wheat, lamb's-ear grasses, and gypsophila are bound to a central core of twisted stub wires and the design is finished with a paper ribbon bow.
Above

is to put the plant materials and any of the desiccants in an airtight tin, close the lid, and set it aside for two, three, or more days, depending on the density and moisture content of the materials to be dried. Very carefully brush or scrape away the desiccant when you think the time is right, and very gently brush it over the plant materials again if you find they are not paper-crisp.

You can speed up the process by drying the plant materials in a desiccant in an oven at the lowest temperature. Layer them in an ovenproof dish of any kind (you needn't use a lid), and process them with the door slightly ajar. If you use silica gel crystals alone, a dish of, say, six peonies should be dry in 20–25 minutes; a mixture of silica gel and any of the other drying agents increases the time factor by about 50%. Check the progress every two or three minutes once you think they should be ready. Over-processing makes the materials unacceptably brittle.

The fastest means of drying plant materials in a desiccant is in a microwave. Layer them in a microwave-proof container – anything (without a lid) from an earthenware or toughened glass dish to a cardboard box – and process on low power. Drying times vary according to the properties of the appliance, the type of container used, and the density and moisture-content of the plants; it is best to experiment, check on progress every minute or so, and make notes of the processing times.

DESICCANT DRYING

1 Fully-opened roses on very short stems and a spray of Singapore orchids are arranged on a layer of silica gel crystals in a microwave-safe dish.

2 The silica gel crystals, which are blue before processing, are sprinkled carefully around and over the flowers. When they are fully covered with the desiccant they can be dried in an oven or a microwave.

As a general guide, a shoe box of six carnations in silica gel crystals dried in the test microwave in seven minutes; four short sprays of delphinium, plus two extra florets, in seven minutes; and four rosebuds, in five minutes. Four short but thick sprays of elaeagnus (silver berry) leaves, also in silica gel, took four minutes to dry, and four short sprays of mimosa flowers and leaves – pretty as fillers in dried arrangements – took four and a half minutes. You may find it preferable to process the materials for a slightly shorter 'cooking' time, and then leave them to dry – but only for five to ten minutes – in the desiccant.

There are good reasons – apart from the sheer joy of being able to unearth perfect dried-flower forms every few minutes – for using one of the above heating methods with desiccants. Since the speeded-up processes utilize the drying agents for a much shorter time, you can quickly preserve a batch of flowers that all come to the peak of perfection at the same time; process wildflowers and

leaves the day you gather them; and dry a treasured composition, a child bridesmaid's headdress for example, before the flowers have time to fade. In such a case, once the flowers are dry you can reassemble them on the circlet or band to keep as a decorative memento.

PREPARATION OF PLANT MATERIAL

Whichever desiccant drying method you choose, you must prepare the flowers and foliage in a similar way. Flower stalks do not respond well to the treatment, and in any case they take up too much space. Imagine the depth of silica gel crystals you would need to dry a fully-opened rose standing upright on a 15cm (6in) stem! Cut individual flowers such as roses, peonies, and pansies to leave short stalks, no more than 1.5cm (½in). Cut flowers with thick calyces, such as carnations and daffodils, just below the calyx, and cut flower sprays like lily-of-the-valley and grape hyacinth (*Muscari*) to leave about 2.5cm (1in) of stalk. If you are using the room temperature or the conventional oven method of desiccant drying, you can, at this stage, push short lengths of stub wire into short, fleshy stems; it makes it easier to wire them onto false stems later. *Please note: you must not use wire of any kind if the materials are to be processed in a microwave.*

Once you have spread a layer of desiccant in the container, position separate flowers upright, so they can be filled most easily with the drying agent, and flower and leaf sprays on their sides. Supporting each upright flower in turn with one hand, spoon the desiccant under it until it takes the shape of the flower; care at this stage makes the difference between average and perfect results. Then sprinkle the desiccant gently, not in a heavy onslaught, over the flower until it is covered. Sprinkle on a covering layer, and process by your preferred method.

A dried-flower panel makes a pleasing impact, whether decorating an exterior wall for a garden party, the back of an unused fireplace, a wall niche, or an arch. The base is made of a double thickness of wire mesh netting enclosing sphagnum moss, and the flowers and seedheads are wired into bunches and hooked into the mesh. **Left**

Restrained use of colour in a floral ring puts the accent on texture. This design, which would be suitable as a desk or table top decoration, includes sage and purple sage, hydrangea and marjoram, and deep red roses and sea lavender arranged on a dry foam ring. **Opposite**

Microwave-drying makes possible a glorious profusion of flowers from all seasons. This creamware mug holds a medley of flowers surrounded by dried foliage sprays. There are roses in various stages of development, carnations and spray carnations, Singapore orchids and freesias, larkspur and mimosa, spray chrysanthemums and daffodils – dried flowers that have to be touched to be believed. **Below**

As you gently brush the desiccant after processing, you should find that the flowers with a strong, deep colour, such as purple Singapore orchids, ruby-red carnations, and dark blue delphinium, have held their colour perfectly. Middle-toned flowers may have faded a little, and some white and pale cream examples, from arum lilies to marguerites, freesias, and primroses, may have turned the delicate colour of parchment. Not all white flowers respond in that way, and some – daisies, dogwood, and candytuft, for example – have been known to emerge dazzling white.

Just how true to colour and how dazzlingly white the materials seem to be at this stage will depend on the type of desiccant used, but they all adhere to the petals and leaves to a greater or lesser extent, covering them with a dusty film. Carefully lift out the preserved materials, which by now will be very brittle, and shake them to remove loose desiccant. Then, using a small camel-hair or similar type of paintbrush, gently brush all the plant surfaces. It can be an exciting revelation when what seemed like a misty grey rose emerges as a wine-red beauty, or what looked like a spray of silver-grey leaves appears with the original green and yellow speckles.

Most plant materials dried in this way, having little or no natural stem, will need to be mounted on false wire stems before being arranged. Details of the various wiring techniques are given later in this book. You can use the flowers in other forms of flowercraft too, attaching them, for example, to a stem ring base to make a floral circlet.

MICROWAVE-DRYING

Open-drying in a microwave is a relatively new technique that can be applied to a range of materials. It is particularly suitable for plants such as gypsophila, lady's mantle, marjoram, tansy, goldenrod, and sedum (stonecrop), which are composed of a mass of florets, and others such as cornflower and feverfew, which are made of a mass of petals. As the flowers dry, the loss of volume and shape is barely discernible. Foliage that dries well by this method includes fennel, sage and purple sage, and silver-leaved types such as santolina, senecio (ground sel), and lavender. This is also a fail-safe way to dry hydrangeas.

Cut the material into sprays of suitable lengths; there is no need to cut off flower stems. Cover the microwave turntable or a suitable plate with a double thickness of kitchen paper towels, and arrange the plant materials in a single layer, no two items touching. To dry cornflowers, for example, you can arrange them in a wheel pattern, heads facing outwards, stems to the middle. Dry the materials on low power for as long as it takes.

In the test microwave, a whole hydrangea head took seven minutes, and retained its pale blue colouring perfectly; a whole head of sedum took six minutes and this, too, kept its colour well; about 12 cornflowers took five minutes and dried very successfully while a plate of short sprays of goldenrod took three minutes.

PRESERVING IN GLYCERIN

Preserving foliage, bracts, and berries in a glycerin and water solution adds a further dimension to a collection of long-lasting plant materials. Branches and small sprays of deciduous evergreen leaves blend well in arrangements with dried flowers and, with their high-gloss appearance, provide an interesting texture contrast. Bracts such as

Arrange dried flowers in natural profusion, and create a design with the appeal of a cottage garden. The materials *include marjoram, love-in-a-mist seedheads, achillea (yarrow), rosebuds, and strawflowers.* **Above**

bells of Ireland have an almost architectural quality, and preserved berries from glossy red rosehips to dense black blackberries retain the warm aura of autumn fruits.

In the preserving process, the glycerin solution is taken up by the stems and carried to every part of the plant material, to the very tip of every leaf. As the water evaporates, the plant cells retain the glycerin, and are held in a decorative state of suspended animation.

Most materials undergo some colour change in the process. Beech leaves, one of the most attractive examples of preserved foliage, turn dark chestnut brown, eucalyptus deepens to a dark gun-metal blue, and laurel leaves become almost black. Bay and rosemary darken only slightly and – an added bonus – retain their scent, while acanthus leaves darken considerably. Most berries shrink a little in the process, a transition barely noticeable in a cluster, and some deepen in tone. Yellow holly berries, for example, turn bright orange, and some red berries mellow to a shade of burnt umber.

If you gather materials throughout the year you can practise a conveyor-belt system of preserving, reusing, and topping up the solution for each successive batch.

To prepare woody stems, scrape the bark about 5cm (2in) from the ends, and split or crush the stem ends so they can most easily take up the preserving liquid. Discard damaged leaves or bracts, and any lower ones that would be trapped in the container.

Make up a solution of one part glycerin, which you can buy from chemists and drugstores, and two parts very hot water. Mix it thoroughly, and pour it into a heatproof container to a depth of about 5cm (2in). Stand the stems in the solution, making sure the ends are submerged. An alternative method, which gives better results with large, fleshy leaves such as acanthus, Japanese fatsia, aspidistra (cast-iron plant), fig, and hosta (plantain lily), is to completely immerse them in a 'bath' of the solution, in a shallow container.

The process time varies according to the size and density of the materials, and it may take anything from three or four days to two or three weeks. When the material is fully preserved, it should be supple, with no traces of brittleness, and have changed colour evenly throughout; it may also show beads of moisture on the surface. If during the process the tips of some leaves start

GLYCERIN PRESERVING

1 Preserving foliage and berries in a glycerin and hot water solution brings them into the almost everlasting category.

2 Large fleshy leaves such as acanthus (shown here), Japanese fatsia, hosta (plantain lily), fig, and some types of ivy are best preserved flat, in a shallow dish, covered with the glycerin and hot water solution.

A rectangular basket is painted purple to match the marjoram that forms the foundation of the arrangement. Wheat and delphinium spires provide the 'points', and peonies, clusters of carthamus, and globe artichoke heads the 'rounds'. Silhouetted against the matt black of the stove, the arrangement makes a lively display all through the summer. **Below**

Dried-flower posies have a natural charm that may be lacking in some formal arrangements. They can hang on any vertical surface from a wall to a door, a bedpost to a chair back. This one is made up of cream rosebuds and lady's mantle with red miniature rosebuds and white sea lavender. **Right**

to dry – which can happen before the solution reaches them – rub the surface on both sides with cotton wool or a tissue soaked in the preservative. And if the plant material takes up the solution before it is fully preserved, top up the container with some more.

When the plant material is preserved, wipe large leaves with a dry cloth to remove any stickiness, and dry the stems thoroughly. Wash and dry leaves that have been immersed. Store the materials upright in dry containers, layered between papers in a box, or hanging in bunches in a cool room, away from strong light. Strain any leftover preserving solution and store it in an airtight bottle for future use.

ADDING TINTS

As stated above, the process of preserving plant materials in a glycerin solution almost invariably brings about a colour change. Some materials, especially leaves, may take on the nearly natural tints and shades of autumn, while others will emerge considerably darker. You may adapt the preserving process and cheat nature still further by adding a little water-soluble dye to the preserving solution, either to intensify natural-looking colours or achieve artificial ones.

Green dye is particularly effective with deciduous leaves such as beech, (but not copper beech), chestnut, oak, and maple, and with ivy and rhododendron, all of which emerge from the treatment with varying shades of deep, rich green and no hint of brown. Copper beech, maple, and eucalyptus leaves take well to a red or rust-coloured dye solution, which turns them copper-bronze, and bells of Ireland bracts and hydrangea flower heads present an opportunity to intensify their appeal with the addition of green, red, or blue colouring.

For a completely different approach and markedly different results, you can add a little bleach to the preserving solution – about one part in ten – to give leaves and bracts a light, bright, sun-drenched look. Sprays of preserved and bleached fern leaves, the colour of pale parchment, are especially pretty in summery arrangements of dried rosebuds and pansies.

Dye can also be added to the water used in one of the air-drying processes. As the plant materials take up the liquid, they also take up the dye, and change colour in the process. You can try the technique with hydrangeas to intensify or exaggerate their natural colour; with gypsophila, which looks especially attractive when dyed pale pink or blue; and with white pearl (pearly) everlasting and sea lavender, whose lack of natural colour gives you a clean palette on which to impose any colour.

Many seedheads are characterized by the modesty and subtlety of their colouring, which can be both attractive in its own right and a foil to more obviously showy dried materials. There may be a time however, when you feel that some seedheads in your collection would benefit from more colour. You can transform mallow stems, their seedpods like small fat stars; lupins (lupines) like silver-grey rabbits' ears; candytuft with whorls of seeds in clusters; dainty stems of grape hyacinths; flat discs of honesty, and many others by dip-dyeing or spraying. This imposed colouring can never be an exact art, since the tones achieved will be influenced by the absorption properties of the various plants and the amount of residual moisture they have retained, but this makes the process all the more fascinating.

For traditional dip-dyeing, you can use a natural dye made from dyers' pokeweed or woad, or, more readily available, onion skins simmered in water to make a brown dye, or even marigold petals – one cup petals and one cup water simmered for an hour to achieve a pale yellow colour. For more vibrant shades and beautiful heathery tones, use the strained and cooled juice from stewed blackberries, mulberries, raspberries, red-currants, and gooseberries (which make a pale, amber-coloured dye). Commercial dyes can also be used. Pour the colorant into jars, or, to dye long stems, shallow trays or baking dishes, and dip in the dried plant materials for a few seconds. It is a mistake to leave them for a long soak; all seedheads are inclined to become soggy. Shake the dyed materials over several layers of newspaper and hang them to dry in a warm, airy room with newspapers underneath them.

After dyeing a few experimental stems, you will discover that the soft and fur-like texture of lupins (lupines) and ballota absorb the colour most readily and emerge with the deepest shades; that Jerusalem sage,

Dip-dyeing is a technique that can be used to give sun-bleached seedheads a new and colourful personality. Natural plant dyes and strained fruit juices, as here, can be used, or commercial dyes can be bought. The secret is to immerse the materials for only a few seconds, and retrieve them before they become soggy. **Above**

knapweed, grape hyacinth, poppy, and teasel are in the medium absorption range; and that honesty takes up the colour only grudgingly and looks as if it has been casually splashed with colour. The 'Colourful Personality' arrangement shows what a dramatic effect can be created with a blend of purple-dyed seedheads and the natural brilliance of Chinese lanterns (winter cherry).

For even more positive results, you can spray dried seedheads and preserved leaves with non-toxic florists' paints, which are available in practically any colour of your choice. If possible, work out of doors, or in a shed or garage. Cover the surface with newspaper, stand the stems upright in a container or hold them in your hand, and spray them all around with light, even strokes. Poppy seedheads can be painted bright scarlet, teasels sprayed a vibrant green, the centres of sunflowers and gaillardia coloured sunshine yellow, and leaves spatter-sprayed metallic gold or silver. The technique opens up new possibilities amounting to a second decorative harvest.

CONTAINERS AND EQUIPMENT

Think of any container you might consider filling to overflowing with fresh flowers, any vase or urn, jug or mug, bowl or basket, can or packet, and then think of some more. That's how varied the possibilities are for dried-flower holders. A container does not have to be waterproof and will not need a moisture-proof liner. It doesn't even have to be a vessel of any kind. You can tie a posy of dried flowers to a wooden spoon or a Polynesian hand brush to make a highly individual decoration for the kitchen; arrange wheat, lavender, strawflowers, and roses in a wire basket lined with moss; and bind dried-flower posies to a hatband for a millinery decoration that will never falter. You can arrange a bundle of Chinese lanterns (winter cherry), ranging from green to orange, in a bundle of bamboo poles, or create a swag of dried flowers, seedheads, cereals, and grasses on a wire frame. By using preformed dry foam shapes available at florists, you can create dried-flower trees with the neatness of topiary;

Spray painting can give dried or fresh plant materials a new and more colourful personality, or bring a sparkle to their appearance. Use non-toxic paints, and work out of doors or close to an open window to minimize the effect of the fumes. **Left**

A kitchen basket, more often used to hold eggs or bread rolls, makes a low-key container for dried flowers. It is lined with sphagnum moss and fitted with dry foam to hold a fan shape of lavender, preserved eucalyptus, wheat, and strawflowers. **Opposite**

Whenever dried flowers and foliage are arranged in stem-holding foam, it should be of the dry, non-absorbent type, which is usually grey or brown and has a sparkly finish. This type is more stable for dried-flower work than absorbent foam used dry (which is not recommended), but the two kinds do share one important feature: they are equally unattractive to look at. Therefore, similar arts of concealment are called for in dried-flower work: short-stemmed flowers recessed into a design and positioned close against the foam; clusters of leaves, or large individual ones, positioned at the base of an arrangement; and snippings – they may be of oats, lady's mantle, or hydrangea – pressed into camouflage service when the design is almost finished. To check there is no likelihood that a glint of foam is showing through, it is a good idea to turn a strong light onto a completed arrangement, or take it to a window, and check it from every angle.

Stems, too, can present another challenge in the matter of concealment. Dried stems, whether they support bunches of air-dried rosebuds or microwave-dried

or compose dried-flower rings, pretty circlets to give as a token for weddings, christenings, and anniversaries.

Most of the equipment, or mechanics, used for fresh-flower arrangements can be applied to dried-flower designs as well. You can fit a jug or vase with a piece cut from a block of stem-holding foam and hold it in place with narrow strips of florists' adhesive tape; press a cylinder of foam into a purpose-made plastic saucer, and secure it with florists' adhesive clay to the neck of a tall container, so that stems may be angled in any direction; and press a piece of foam onto the prongs of a plastic spike fixed to a wooden board or shallow dish. You can tape or wire a piece of foam to a woven placemat and arrange dried flowers for a wall decoration, or bind dried-flower posies with florists' silver wire and press them into a vine wreath form or other ring shape with staples cut from stub wires. Tape a piece of foam to the handle of a basket, and trail dried flowers and leaves to follow the curve, or use foam to secure a nosegay to the neck of a bottle.

cornflowers, may have lost some of their original colour and characteristics, but they are natural and will pass in a crowd. But false wire stems, even when wrapped in all-enveloping bands of gutta percha (floral) tape, can look unacceptably harsh and need to be kept out of sight.

To meet this requirement, you simply have to arrange the dried flowers and foliage in close proximity, the way they would appear in a well-stocked flower border. You could dry all the flowers and foliage sprays in desiccants in a microwave, and mount all the flowers, and many of the leaf sprays on stub wires.

To create a more open design, and still not reveal the secret of the false stems, you can arrange a foundation of foliage and flower sprays as in the 'Candle Glow' arrangement, and conceal the wire-mounted materials – the roses, carnations, and anemones – among them.

Another solution is to use dried natural stems such as wheat or rye as false stems for other dried materials. Simply push the short stem of a cluster of hydrangea florets or a strawflower into the hollow stalk to elevate the plant material to new and natural-looking heights. The 'Birthday Basket' arrangement shows how decorative and visually acceptable wheat stalks can be.

POSIES, SWAGS, AND WREATHS

A free-style bunch of papery flowers comprising a country-style wall or table decoration; a dried-flower posy adorning the bride's chair at a wedding; an elegant floral ribbon outlining the top table at a family celebration party; a hay-covered ring studded with the brightest and boldest dried flowers imaginable; a vine wreath form covered with scented lavender – preserved materials have a variety of roles to play in the composition of bunches, posies, swags, and wreaths.

On the spur of the moment, you can gather a handful of dried flowers into a sheaf or bunch that has a casual, unstudied charm. Place the longest stems flat on a work surface, cover them with dried flower heads in diminishing ranks, arrange a few wayward stems to give width and wispiness at the sides, bind the stems with twine, raffia or florists' silver wire, and finish the design with a raffia or ribbon bow. Hanging bunches such as this find a decorative place in the hallway, kitchen, living room, or bedroom according to the materials you choose. They can be designed, too, with an air of calculated informality, to grace the most formal of occasions, such as a wedding.

A posy or bouquet to be carried by a bride or her bridesmaids calls for more attention to detail, and in many cases the flowers will need to be wired. This technique not only serves the purpose of mounting short-stemmed dried materials onto false wire stems, but also lends flexibility to the design – you can bend wire stems in a manner not possible with natural ones – and minimizes the girth and clumsiness of the handle. The project for a bridal bouquet included here, a pretty cascade of dried and wired roses, orchids, statice, strawflowers, carnations, and hydrangea, is designed to become a romantic family heirloom in the Victorian tradition.

Floral ribbons and swags are in keeping with a much longer tradition, that of enhancing the setting for a special occasion – whether a wedding or a festival – with garlands of flowers. By using dried and preserved flowers and foliage you can compose a garland gradually, and well in advance of the occasion, adding to it whenever you have a few moments to spare. Best of all, dried-flower garlands will retain their good looks whatever the weather and however long the celebrations last, and afterwards they can be carefully packed away and stored until the next occasion arises.

The core material used, the hidden thread around which the garland is composed, will depend on the weight and volume of the decorative materials. You can use tightly coiled paper ribbon, florists' silver wire or thicker gauges, fine twine, string, cord, or rope. Just as for fresh-flower garlands, you may choose to conceal the core beneath a wrapping of dry hay or sphagnum moss, or bind on a foundation of readily-available (and in this case dried or preserved) foliage.

To outline the edge of the wedding cake table or the top table at the reception, you might compose a summery-looking garland on a core of unfurled paper ribbon, in a colour that matches or complements the overall scheme chosen by the bride. If you were given enough advance notice, you might even have the opportunity to dye some plant materials, such as sea lavender or gypsophila, especially for the occasion.

Small posy baskets of dried
rosebuds, lavender, and
gypsophila – pretty decorations
for a dressing table – would
make thoughtful gifts for
friends of all generations.
Opposite

Wiring dried flowers

1 To bind a flower which has a reasonable length of stem, such as the air-dried rose and the delphinium shown here, place a stub wire close against the stem and bind the two together with silver wire.

You Will Need

stub wires ● roll of florists' silver wire ● wire cutters ● florists' scissors ● gutta percha (floral) tape ● scissors

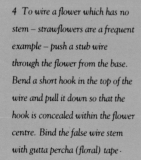

2 To cover the false wire stem, wrap one end of a length of gutta percha (floral) tape around both the rose stem and the wire. Holding the wire in one hand and the tape in the other, twist the flower so that the tape is wrapped around the wire. Each twist of the tape should overlap and stick to the previous one. Fasten off the tape just before the end of the wire.

3 To wire dried flowers which have very short stems, such as the ranunculus shown here, which was dried in silica gel crystals, place a stub wire close against the short stem length and bind them together with silver wire. Bind the false wire stem with gutta percha (floral tape) as described.

4 To wire a flower which has no stem – strawflowers are a frequent example – push a stub wire through the flower from the base. Bend a short hook in the top of the wire and pull it down so that the hook is concealed within the flower centre. Bind the false wire stem with gutta percha (floral) tape.

For a decoration on a larger scale, to drape across a church or barn door at a harvest festival or Thanksgiving, you could wrap a length of rope with hay (green twine is a suitable binding material) and tie on bunches of oats, wheat, dried vine leaves, and dahlias. If you use several strands of raffia or twist them into slender plaits finished with straggly bows, the ties can form an attractive part of the overall design.

As the 'Midsummer Hay Ring' illustrates, the hay can be revealed to decorative advantage, and it is not necessary to cover it completely with the decorative materials. This ring, which could convey the brightest of welcomes to guests arriving for a barbecue or garden party, is composed on a double copper-wire ring form, available from florists. The flowers are formed into bunches, bound with silver wire, and attached to the ring with staples made from bent stub wires.

Wire ring forms, which are more useful than decorative, do need concealing. You can do this in a number of ways to create floral rings for a variety of moods. Bind the ring with natural or coloured raffia, and attach dried herbs like fennel, marjoram, bay and sage, bunches of dried chillies, and heads of garlic for a practical kitchen decoration. Or bind the ring with paper ribbon, attach dried-flower posies or individual flower heads, and finish the design with a flourish with a large paper bow. It's a delightful notion for a nursery or young girl's room.

Vine wreath forms and those made of twisted willow or grass stems, all available from florists, have natural credentials, and may be fully or partly covered with decorative materials. You can attach bunches of lavender and a cluster of strawflowers to a trio of bleached willow rings, a minimal but aromatic decoration suitable for a bathroom, or cover a vine wreath with overlapping lavender bunches and dried-flower posies until the base is no more than a hidden asset.

Dry foam rings, available in sizes from 15cm (6in) to 30cm (12in) in diameter, call for a different technique. Here is a chance to use dried flowers, seedheads, and leaves on the shortest of stems, or, if you use clear, quick-setting adhesive or hot glue, ones with no stem at all. To make a thoughtful christening gift you could cover a ring with snippings of sea lavender and tansy, goldenrod and delphinium, love-in-a-mist and marjoram, and arrange a few rosebuds at intervals. Or, for a harvest decoration, outline a ring with short sprays of oats, and pack it with colourful strawflowers and seedheads to display on a door or wall, or to edge a rugged basket.

POTPOURRI

In days gone by large country households employed a mistress of the potpourri, who had the enviable task of composing aromatic blends of dried petals, leaves, spices, and oils, some displayed in decorative bowls and others sewn into fine linen, to scent the rooms and mask unwelcome odours. Today, although we no longer have this underlying need for potpourri, the therapeutic joy of composing an individual perfume from flowers gathered in the garden or saved from a gift bouquet is as compelling as ever.

There are two basic types of potpourri, one made by the 'moist' and the other by the 'dry' method. In the past, rose petals were at the heart of both, since Provence and cabbage roses grew in abundance in Elizabethan gardens, and their petals held their fragrance for many months. Today, as potpourri grows in popularity, the dry type may be made from any blend of dried materials, chosen as

Celebrate the harvest with a ring of oats, strawflowers, rosebuds, and love-in-a-mist seedheads. It could be used to add personality to a collection of baskets, hung on a door or a wall, or propped up as the centre-piece of a buffet table.
Above

much for their colour and texture as for their odour. Any lack in this latter quality can be compensated for by the addition of more essential oils and spices.

THE MOIST METHOD

Traditional moist potpourri is made with rose petals dried in the sun (or oven) until they are leathery, but not crisp. The petals are packed into a moisture-proof box (not a tin) between layers of coarse salt – three cups of petals to one of salt – and are covered with a lid and set aside for ten days. During this time the salt will draw out the remaining moisture from the petals, and the mixture will first ferment and then form a block. Now the creative part of the process begins. Break up the block into a jar or crock, stir in 45g (3tbsp) of a mixture of ground spices such as allspice, cinnamon, cloves, mace, and nutmeg, and 45g (3tbsp) ground orris-root powder as a fixative, which you can buy in healthfood stores.

Cover the container and set it aside, except for a daily stir, for six weeks, then stir in two or three drops of an essential plant oil such as rose oil (attar of roses), rose geranium, or bergamot oil. Cover and store for a further two weeks before using. For visual variety, you can substitute marigold, larkspur, carnation, peony, or other petals for a proportion of the rose petals, or stir in a few rosebuds or chamomile flowers when you add the oils.

THE DRY METHOD

The dry method of making potpourri uses, as the term indicates, fully-dried petals, flowers, herbs, and leaves. These and other plant materials, such as tiny cones, wood shavings, and whole spices, are mixed with ground spices, orris-root, and essential oils, covered and then stirred once a day for six weeks. There are no hard and fast rules about quantities and proportions, but an allowance of 30–45g (2–3 tbsp) ground spices, 30g (2tbsp) ground orris-root powder, 10g (2tsp) dried lemon, orange, or lime peel, and two drops essential oil to every four cups of dried plant material makes a pleasantly balanced mixture.

Exactly how you dry the plant material is a matter of choice. The traditional method involves spreading out the petals, flowers, and leaves on a woven tray, and leaving it in a shady spot in the garden to dry in the heat of the sun. Instead, you can take as examples a handful of sweet-scented lily-of-the-valley flowers picked from the stalks or lemon verbena leaves, spread them in a single layer on a baking tray, and dry them for two or three days in a warm cupboard, or about half an hour in an oven at the lowest temperature and with the door slightly ajar. Or you can spread the materials on a microwave-safe plate or dish and dry them in a microwave at low power for about 10–12 minutes. Stir the materials from the sides of the tray inwards every couple of minutes, remove when crisp

A variety of floral ring decorations composed on vine wreath forms, dry foam rings, and twisted willow rings. They can harmonize with any room scheme using inexpensive materials like grasses, oats, and other seedheads, through honesty, strawflowers, and statice to more precious materials such as dried rosebuds and delphinium. **Opposite**

Potpourri, which is both an environmental perfume and a design accessory, can be displayed in open bowls, baskets or, as here, in stylish ornaments. **Left**

POTPOURRI RECIPES

Cottage Garden mix
(dry method)

1 cup dried lavender flowers
1 cup dried rose petals
1 cup dried pinks (Dianthus)
1 cup dried scented geranium leaves
15g (1tbsp) ground cinnamon
10g (2tsp) ground allspice
5g (1tsp) dried grated lemon peel
30g (2tbsp) dried orris-root powder
2 drops rose oil

Mix ingredients together in a covered container, and set aside for six weeks. Stir daily to distribute the fragrances.

Woodland mix
(dry method)

1 cup dried lime seedpods, or 'keys'
1 cup cedar bark shavings
1 cup sandalwood shavings
1 cup small cones
15g (1tbsp) whole cloves
15g (1tbsp) star anise
1 stick cinnamon, crushed
30g (2tbsp) dried orris-root powder
3 drops sandalwood oil

Mix ingredients together in a covered container and set aside for six weeks. Stir the contents daily to distribute the spices evenly.

Wedding bouquet mix
(dry method)

1 cup dried lily-of-the-valley flowers
1 cup dried white fuchsia flowers
1 cup dried white miniature roses
1 cup dried lavender leaves, crumbled
45g (3tbsp) dried orris-root powder
4 drops neroli (orange blossom oil)
4 drops lily-of-the-valley oil

This recipe does not use ground spices, as they would colour the white blossoms. Mix ingredients together in a lidded container. Stir every day for six weeks.

and papery, and allow to dry completely before putting into a lidded container.

You can store dried materials from one season to the next, ready to compose unseasonal and year-round potpourri blends, or use dried flowers and leaves from your plant collection. A single stem of air-dried larkspur, for example, can yield a wealth of bright blue florets, a bunch of deep pink cornflowers can add a colourful spark to a rose-petal mixture, and sprigs of air-dried purple sage add pungency to a potpourri garden blend of lavender, pinks, and carnations.

USING POTPOURRI

If your potpourri loses a little of its aroma over a period of time, it can be revived. Simply stir in another two or three drops of essential oil. And if the mixture loses its colour sharpness – as it will if set out in an open bowl in sunlight – just stir in a few dried miniature rosebuds, santolina flowers, tansy clusters, and the like.

Potpourri presents a delightful range of display options: open bowls to be stirred with the fingers to release the blended aromas; perforated 'pomander' bowls, porcelain or woven baskets – especially attractive with woodland mixtures of cones, bark, and sandalwood shavings; and cotton bags, sachets, and pillows to scent wardrobes and linen cupboards. An effective display can be made by filling a glass container with carnation and rose petal potpourri and placing it next to a profusion of dried garden flowers. Or cover a dry foam ring with glue and press on a golden potpourri blend of, say, forsythia and fuchsia flowers, marigold petals, and crushed lemon balm leaves. Both are romantic and pretty notions that demonstrate the versatility of petal power.

PRESSED FLOWERCRAFT

Pressing flowers and leaves between sheets of absorbent paper brings back memories of childhood, of sitting in a field and arranging buttercups and frondy grasses in heavy books. The key elements to success in this single-plane method of preserving are adequate moisture absorption, which is best provided by blotting paper, though smooth-surfaced kitchen paper and tissues are also suitable; a heavy weight or pressure, which can be achieved by pressing materials between pages in a large book, or in a flower press; a warm, dry atmosphere; and patience.

To be sure your pressed materials retain their original colours, it is important to change the absorbent papers

The traditional way to press flowers and leaves – between sheets of absorbent paper in a heavy book. The photograph shows (top to bottom) phlox flowers, carnation petals, alkanet (anchusa) flowers, and herb Robert stems. **Left**

two or three times during the first few days (and dry them for reuse). Then set the pressing medium aside and leave undisturbed for at least six months.

Deciding where to start, and which flowers, leaves, and grasses to press, can be one of the most delightfully overwhelming of all flowercraft choices. Wandering around a garden, snipping flowers, leaves, and even weeds from borders and flowerbeds can yield enough material to compose a pressed-flower posy, recreate a garden scene, or arrange an abstract design for months to come. You can gather materials from the countryside (though be sure they are not protected plants), give them a reviving drink when you get home, and press them for posterity. Or preserve flowers, petals, and foliage from a bunch bought from a market stall or – more nostalgically – a treasured gift bouquet.

It may seem like stating the obvious, but success relies on every part of the plant material coming into contact with the drying medium – the blotting paper. For this reason, it is essential to press materials of equal thickness on a single page. For this reason, too, thick-centred flowers, such as spray chrysanthemums, give disappointing results when pressed whole; the petals that do not make regular contact with the paper are likely to discolour and wither.

The trick with all such flowers – marigolds, gerberas, carnations, zinnias, roses, and many others – is to pull off each petal and press it separately. A single flower will then yield a multitude of petals, which can be reassembled more sparingly to create an image of the original. Trumpet-shaped flowers such as daffodils, freesias, and Peruvian lilies may be sliced in half vertically, using the sharp blade of a craft knife, and each half pressed separately, providing two for the price of one. Flat flowers such as pansies, primulas, borage, daisies, and hydrangea florets should be snipped off just below the calyces, and the pretty heads of umbellifers such as sheep's parsley

POTPOURRI INGREDIENTS

1 *A handful of rose and carnation petals on a woven tray is set to dry by the most natural process of all – in the heat of the sun. Avoid placing petals in the full glare of the sun; a warm but shady place is best. Petals should be brought in before evening, when the dew would spoil them.*

2 *Ingredients which can be used to make potpourri. From the left, dried rosemary, lavender, and bay leaves, dried ground orris-root powder, dried rosemary leaves, a selection of essential oils, ground cinnamon, dried chillies and cinnamon sticks, whole cloves, a blend of dried flowers, and limes and lemons. The dried peel of citrus fruit is finely grated or chopped for use in the spice mixture.*

Pressing flower petals as you gather them adds to the pleasure of the craft. The flower press is arranged with a pattern of sweet pea flowers, spray chrysanthemum petals, and ranunculus petals. **Left**

Pressed pansies, one of the most successful flowers to preserve in this way, were later arranged in a ring to create a Victorian-style decoration. Here, they are pressed between sheets of blotting paper in a flower press, and are shown with surgical tweezers for handling. **Opposite**

(Queen Anne's lace) and wild carrot may be pressed whole or as separate clusters, when they look like snowflakes. Short sprays of delicate flowers like forget-me-not, speedwell, and lady's mantle give variety to future designs. With this ultimate goal in mind, it is a good idea to press some buds, such as buttercups and daisies, and naturally curving stalks, such as those of clematis and, again, buttercup.

Pressed foliage is as essential to many representational compositions as it is to arrangements of fresh and dried flowers, and it is useful to have a selection of leaves chosen as much for their shape as for their colour. Clover, sheep's parsley, and aquilegia (columbine), with their delicate shapes; feathery fennel and cosmos; slender wallflower, willow, and lavender; heart-shaped geranium and ivy; and fallen leaves in all their shape and colour variety – there is so much design potential to press and store for future use.

Once flowers and leaves have been pressed, they will, like all dried materials, be brittle and damage-prone. Handle them carefully with plastic tweezers or surgical tweezers, and keep them in a warm, dry environment, in transparent packets. Use a small paintbrush (preferably camel-hair) to position them in the design, and fasten in place with an opaque glue applied sparingly at intervals with the tip of a wooden cocktail stick. Cover each flower after gluing with a piece of clean white paper, and gently press it in place. When you are overlapping petals, flowers, and leaves, allow the glue of one layer to dry before imposing the next. When you have to leave the work overnight or when it has been completed, cover with a sheet of paper and then glass or a board weighed down with a heavy object to keep it flat.

Pressed-flower designs can be as simple or as creative and involved as you please. You can compose a small spray of flowers and leaves to make a gift tag or a greetings card; an alphabetical sampler to commemorate a baby's birth; a gentle curve of primulas, heather, and fern to complement an oval frame; or build up a realistic flower design using pressed grasses to represent a basket with flowers, buds, leaves, and stalks cascading in country-style profusion. Why not turn back the clock and create a cardboard ring of pressed pansies in the Victorian tradition, or compose a hoop of pressed autumn leaves and dried seedpods.

PRESSED FLOWERCRAFT EQUIPMENT

The makings of pressed-flower pictures, greetings cards, gift tags and labels: pressed flowers and leaves stored in transparent boxes and envelopes, children's craft glue and wooden cocktail sticks to apply it, surgical tweezers, a small paintbrush, scissors, a ruler, and iron-on transparent covering.

Whatever your choice of design may be, and whatever the end product you create, all pressed-flower compositions must be protected from dust and damage. Cover greetings cards and tags with film wrap, and pictures with glass or transparent iron-on mounts. To prevent colour fading, display all pressed-flower work away from strong light, especially direct sunlight.

DESIGNER FLOWERS

So far we have discussed ways of capturing the beauty of the flower garden in terms of drying, preserving, and pressing techniques – ways of holding plant materials in a state of decorative suspended animation. But alongside all the cultivated blooms in the florists' shops – and almost indistinguishable except at very close range – there is another colourful and long-lasting crop, that of 'designer' flowers. Often referred to as 'silk' flowers – although most are made of washable synthetic materials – artificial flowers crop up in all shapes and sizes. There is even a relatively new range that simulates dried flowers, of which the dried roses are especially convincing.

You can use designer flowers, which are mounted on stout wires, as you would dried ones, arranging them in dry stem-holding foam or anchoring them in a container fitted with crumpled wire mesh netting. If you find the wire stems are considerably longer than you need for your arrangement, just bend them back, to avoid shortening them permanently, and insert the double thickness of wire into the container.

Designer flowers make perfect partners for preserved materials. You can arrange a lavish-looking bunch of towering delphiniums and powder-blue hydrangeas with preserved copper-bronze beech leaves in a basket in the hearth; compose a meadow posy of cornflowers, poppies, and daisies with dried grasses to display in a sparkling glass or silver container on the dining table; or use scarlet designer poinsettias and carnations with fresh or preserved evergreens on a pedestal to decorate a church over the Christmas holidays.

You can display the made flowers in the steamiest of bathrooms and kitchens; a glass jug of white lilies would look stylish in the first instance, and a stone jar of narcissus and marigolds in the other. And for a lasting gift, you could arrange a basket of designer flowers, peonies, hydrangeas, roses, and statice. It would be a perfect token to celebrate a baby's birth or baptism, or to give to a friend who would especially appreciate the 'no watering needed' aspect of fabric flowers.

A pressed flower design in the Victorian tradition – a ring of pansies stuck in overlapping circles onto a piece of cardboard. The circlet would make a delightful decoration for a bedroom, whether it was mounted in an old frame, protected under a piece of glass on a table or dressing table, or covered with iron-on transparent plastic sheeting and hung on a wide ribbon over a bed. **Right**

Sometimes dinner- and teaware is just too pretty for mere eating and drinking! This posy-patterned milk jug is arranged with a selection of dried and dyed plant materials in a scheme reminiscent of old pink velvet. **Opposite**

PRESERVING PLANT MATERIALS

The following table is a guide to some of the many plant materials you can preserve. It is not, and could not possibly be, a comprehensive list, but should help you select the appropriate method for any plant of your choice.

Plant material	Part of plant	Method
Acanthus	flower	air-drying
	leaf	glycerin
	seedhead	air-drying
Achillea (yarrow)	flower	air-drying
Anemone	flower	desiccant
Asparagus	leaf	microwave
Aspidistra (cast-iron plant)	leaf	glycerin
Astilbe (spiraea)	flower	air-drying
Bay	leaf	desiccant, glycerin
Beech	leaf	glycerin
Bell heather	flower	air-drying
Bells of Ireland	bract	air-drying, glycerin
Blackberry	leaf and berry	glycerin
Broom	short flower spray	desiccant
Bulrush	seedhead	air-drying
Buttercup	flower	desiccant
Camellia	flower	desiccant
Campion	flower	air-drying
Candytuft	flower	desiccant
	seedhead	air-drying
Caraway	seedhead	air-drying
Carnation	flower	desiccant
Celosia (cockscomb)	flower	air-drying
Chamomile	flower	air-drying, air-drying in water
Chestnut	leaf	glycerin
Chinese lantern (winter cherry)	seedhead	air-drying
Chive	flower	air-drying
Choisya	leaf	glycerin
Chrysanthemum	flower	desiccant
Clarkia	flower	air-drying
Clematis	leaf and seedhead	air-drying
Copper beech	leaf	air-drying, glycerin
Cornflower	flower	air-drying, air-drying in water, microwave
Corn cob (Indian corn)	seedhead	air-drying
Cow parsley (cow parsnip)	seedhead	air-drying
Daffodil	flower	desiccant
Dahlia	flower	desiccant
Daisy	flower	desiccant
Delphinium	flower	air-drying, desiccant
Dock	seedhead	air-drying
Dogwood	seedhead	air-drying
Dryandra	flower	air-drying
Elaeagnus (silver berry)	leaf	glycerin, microwave
Eryngium (sea holly)	flower	air-drying
Eucalyptus	leaf	glycerin
Fennel	leaf	air-drying, microwave
	seedhead	air-drying
Fern	leaf	glycerin
Fescue grass	seedhead	air-drying
Feverfew	flower	air-drying, air-drying in water, microwave
Fig	leaf	glycerin
Forsythia	short flower sprays	desiccant
Foxglove	flower	desiccant
Freesia	flower	desiccant
Gaillardia	seedhead	air-drying
Geranium	leaf, flower	desiccant
Giant hogweed	seedhead	air-drying
Globe amaranth	flower	air-drying
Globe artichoke	seedhead	air-drying
Goldenrod	flower	air-drying, microwave
Grape hyacinth	flower	desiccant
Gypsophila	flower	air-drying, air-drying in water, microwave
Hare's-tail grass	seedhead	air-drying
Heather	flower	air-drying
Holly	leaf	glycerin
Hollyhock	flower	desiccant
Honesty	seedhead	air-drying
Hop	leaf, bract	air-drying, glycerin
Hosta	leaf	glycerin
Hyacinth	flower	desiccant
Hydrangea	flower, bract	air-drying, air-drying in water, microwave

Ivy	leaf	glycerin
Japanese fatsia	leaf	glycerin
Jerusalem sage	flower, leaf, seedhead	air-drying
Knapweed	seedhead	air-drying
Laburnum	short flower sprays	desiccant
Lady's mantle	flower	air-drying, microwave
Larkspur	flower	air-drying, desiccant
Laurel	leaf	glycerin
Lavender	flower	air-drying, air-drying in water
	leaf	microwave
Lilac	small flower sprays	desiccant
Lily	flower	desiccant
Lily-of-the-valley	flower	desiccant
Linseed (flaxseed)	seedhead	air-drying
London pride (saxifrage)	flower	desiccant
Love-in-a-mist	flower, seedhead	air-drying
Love-lies-bleeding	seedhead	air-drying
Lupin (lupine)	flower	desiccant
	seedhead	air-drying
Magnolia	flower	desiccant
Mallow	flower	desiccant
	seedhead	air-drying
Maple	leaf	glycerin
Marguerite	flower	desiccant
Marjoram	flower	air-drying, microwave
Millet	seedhead	air-drying
Mimosa	flower sprays	desiccant, air-drying, air-drying in water
Mullein	seedhead	air-drying
Narcissus	flower	desiccant
Oak	leaf	glycerin
Oats	seedhead	air-drying
Old man's beard (Clematis vitalba, C. virginiana)	leaf, seedhead	air-drying
Onion	seedhead	air-drying
Orchid	flower	desiccant
Pampas grass	seedhead	air-drying
Pansy	flower	desiccant
Pearl (pearly) everlasting	flower	air-drying, air-drying in water
Peony	flower	air-drying, desiccant
Pine	cone	air-drying
Pink (button carnation)	flower	air-drying, desiccant
Polyanthus	flower	desiccant
Poppy	seedhead	air-drying
Pot marigold	flower	air-drying, desiccant
Primula (primrose)	flower	desiccant
Quaking grass	seedhead	air-drying
Ranunculus	flower	desiccant
Rhododendron	leaf	glycerin, microwave
Rose	bud, flower, leaf fully-opened	air-drying
	flower	desiccant
	hip	glycerin
Rosemary	leaf	glycerin, microwave
Rue	seedhead	air-drying
Sage	flower	air-drying
	leaf	air-drying, microwave
Santolina	leaf	air-drying, microwave
Sea lavender	flower	air-drying, air-drying in water
Sedge	seedhead	air-drying
Sedum (stonecrop)	flower	microwave
Senecio (groundsel)	leaf	air-drying, microwave
Silver-leaved everlasting	flower	air-drying
Sorrel	seedhead	air-drying
Statice	flower	air-drying
Stock	flower	desiccant
Strawflower	flower	air-drying
Sunflower	seedhead	air-drying
Sunray (swan river) everlasting	flower	air-drying
Sweet pea	flower	desiccant
Tansy	flower	air-drying, microwave
Teasel	seedhead	air-drying
Thistle	seedhead	air-drying
Timothy grass	seedhead	air-drying
Vine	leaf	desiccant
Wallflower	flower	desiccant
Wheat	seedhead	air-drying
Winged everlasting	flower	air-drying
Zinnia	flower	desiccant

BIRTHDAY BASKET

You Will Need

flat rectangular basket ● plastic prong ● florists' adhesive clay ● dry stem-holding foam ● scissors ● florists' scissors ● selection of dried flowers such as larkspur, strawflowers, sea lavender, peonies, statice, and rosebuds ● bundle of wheat stalks ● 2.5cm- (1in-) wide satin ribbon ● half a stub wire

A 'posy' of dried flowers makes a thoughtful and long-lasting gift for a birthday, anniversary, or other celebration. It is a design with an illusory secret – which is revealed in the step-by-step photographs.

1 Choose a basket with a rugged texture, which contrasts well with the delicacy of the flowers and serves as an effective frame. The flowers range from deep pink through coral and pale mauve to dark blue.

2 Fix the plastic prong with a strip of clay, just off-centre in the base of the basket and press a piece of dry foam onto it. Cut short lengths of spiky flowers – blue larkspur, for example – and position to make a fan shape.

3 Complete the outline of larkspur, then fill in the shape with short stems of statice and rosebuds. Begin a row of strawflowers to give more visual weight close to the centre.

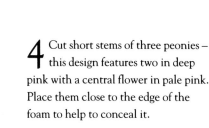

4 Cut short stems of three peonies – this design features two in deep pink with a central flower in pale pink. Place them close to the edge of the foam to help to conceal it.

5 Now comes the illusion. Cut the wheat stalks in a range of lengths so that some will extend just beyond the rim of the basket and others will fall somewhat shorter. Push the stalks into the foam so that they form a broad, thick fan shape.

6 Fill in the floral posy with sprigs of sea lavender to soften the outline and extend beyond the basket rim. Tie a bow with the ribbon, trim the ends at a slant and push the stub wire through the back of the loop. Bend the wire into a U-shape and press it into the foam between the peonies. Fill in any gaps with more sea lavender.

FLORAL TRIM

You Will Need

core material such as coiled paper ribbon, string, or cord ● roll of florists' silver wire ● selection of dried flowers such as statice, sea lavender, marjoram, delphinium, and strawflowers ● paper ribbon for bow ● pin, for fixing

A ribbon of dried flowers outlining the rim of a party table creates an air of festivity. You can compose the decoration in advance, confident that it will retain its crisp and colourful personality no matter how sultry the weather may be. And when the party's over you can pack the floral ribbon away until the next time.

1 A design of this kind, which is composed of short-stemmed posies, can be made up of clippings of dried flowers left over from other designs. It is a good idea to save all such materials in a box for this purpose. Here, coiled paper ribbon forms the core material, in a colour to tone with the flowers.

2 Make up small posies – varied or colour coordinated according to preference. Each posy in this design includes a strawflower to give it definition. Bind the stems with silver wire and cut to an even length.

3 Measure and cut the length of core required. Beginning close to one end of the core material, bind on the first posy with the flower heads towards the end of the coil. Bind on more posies, the heads of each one covering the stems of the one before.

216

4 When you have completed the floral ribbon, pin it at intervals to the tablecloth. Make one or two large bows from the paper ribbon and pin to the cloth.

5 A bird's-eye view of the decorated table, the floral ring highlighted by generous paper ribbon bows.

DESIGNER TREE

Blossoming with strong primary colours set off by crisp white, this indoor tree makes a natural link between the garden and the home, and looks equally good in a doorway, on a windowsill, or a table.

1 The flowerpot may be painted with white emulsion to give the design a lighter, less earthy look. Select a ribbon that combines the colours of the flowers. Red, white, and blue gingham looks fresh and crisp.

2 Press a strip of adhesive clay onto the base of the plastic prong, fix it in the base of the pot and push a ball of modelling or self-hardening clay firmly onto it. Insert the twig and press the clay around it to hold it in place. Push the dry foam spheres onto the twig.

3 Cut short the flower stems – the shorter they are, the fewer you will need to cover the spheres and conceal the foam. Cover the first sphere with flowers in alternating colours, such as blue and white. Fill any remaining gaps.

4 Cover the second sphere in a
similar way, using short stems of
statice close to the foam and longer,
wispy materials to provide a softer
outline. Position a few rosebuds or
other feature flowers at intervals among
the statice. Tie a ribbon bow just below
the higher sphere.

5 Tie more ribbons close to the pot,
to trail over the rim. Instead of a
multi-coloured check design, narrow
ribbon or tape in each of the three
principal flower colours may be used.
Cover the holding material in the pot
with dry moss.

RED, BRIGHT AND BLUE

A bundle of sun-bleached hogweed stems with their deep vertical ridges makes a highly textured holder for a colourful bunch of dried roses and larkspur. The stems were arranged in a rotund glass goldfish bowl, but they could be tied with raffia or paper ribbon and displayed, free-standing, as natural stem vases.

1 Bleached to a pale silver-grey, the hogweed stems make a dramatic foil for dried flowers in a vibrant colour range. Other suitable hollow stems, many of which may be found in the wild, are cow parsley (cow parsnip), wild parsnip, and hollyhock.

2 The sharp blade of a craft knife is best to cut the stems without splitting or tearing them. Cut them to more or less equal lengths so that they will extend a little above the rim of the container. Any side shoots on the stems will add interest to the composition. Gather the stems into a bundle, lower them into the container and twist so they have a circular slant.

3 Using each hogweed stem as a separate holder, position a row of larkspur stems, of uneven lengths, at the back of the design. Partly cover them with touches of fiery red. Dyed materials work well in this context.

4 Add some bottle brush stems, and then the foreground material – the dried roses complete with their leaves, and dark red strawflowers.

5 Unfurl a length of printed paper ribbon from both ends. Wrap the tightly-coiled centre section twice around the neck of the bowl and neaten the ends by cutting at a slant.

CANDLE GLOW

You Will Need

shallow bowl or dish ● *plastic prong*
● *florists' adhesive clay* ● *dry*
stem-holding foam ● *2 plastic*
candle spikes ● *2 candles of*
unequal length ● *selection of dried*
flowers and foliage (see above)
● *florists' scissors*

Fully-opened roses and dense, petally carnations; exotic Singapore orchids and creamy madonna lilies; dainty spray carnations and deep purple anemones; sprays of fluffy mimosa and two-coloured elaeagnus – all the flowers and foliage in this cottage-style candle arrangement were dried in silica gel crystals in a microwave.

1 A shallow bowl on a short foot, lifting it just above the table top, helps to emphasize the inverted curve shape of the design. Choose candles in a neutral shade, or one that will not overshadow the delicate creamy tints of some of the flowers.

2 Press a short strip of florists' adhesive clay onto the base of the plastic prong, press it into the centre of the dish and push the foam block onto it. Push the candle spikes into the foam, one at each end. Tapering to a narrow point, these spikes do not break up the foam as a candle may do.

3 Position the candles in the two plastic holders and build up the design around them. Select sprays of a curving plant material such as dried broom and position with a few mimosa sprays to outline a deep, upward curve. Cover the holders on both sides with short sprays of dried variegated leaves.

4 Follow the outline of the foliage with slender flower sprays such as purple and cream Singapore orchids. Place larger, more rounded dried flowers such as carnations and roses close to the foam on all sides. Fill in the gaps with more roses and rosebuds.

5 Complete the design by grouping deep-coloured flowers in a cluster at the centre, and arranging small flowers such as spray carnations in threes and fours for maximum impact. Check that there are no flowers or leaves too close to the candle flames.

MIDSUMMER HAY RING

Celebrate the height of summer with a dried flower hay ring composed of all the bright and beautiful colours of the rainbow. It can be hung as a brilliant party welcome on a gate, or an outside wall, or use it as a table decoration that will have guests reaching for their sunglasses.

1 A 'dished' type of copper-wire ring, which has the inner circle slightly lower than the outer one, is better for a design of this type, as it is easier to bind a deep layer of hay or moss. Choose ribbons that match the flowers as closely as possible for a fully coordinated look.

2 Tie the twine to the outer circle of the ring. Place handfuls of hay or moss over the ring and bind it on securely, taking the twine over and through the ring and pulling it tightly, to conceal it in the covering material. When the ring is completely covered, cut the twine and tie it to the ring.

3 Gather the flowers into small mixed posies, mixing the colours for the brightest effect. Cut the stems short and bind them with silver roll wire. Make several posies in this way.

4 Cut several stub wires in half and bend them to make U-shaped staples. Place a posy over the hay-covered ring, loop a staple over the stems and press into the hay. Bend back the wire ends and twist them around the back of the wire ring to secure.

5 Placez un grand nombre de petits bouquets autour de la couronne en prenant soin que les têtes de chacun d'entre eux recouvrent les tiges du précédent. Alternez les couleurs pour obtenir un plus bel effet en associant par exemple des bleuets bien vifs et des immortelles à bractées orange.

6 Vous pouvez soit recouvrir entièrement la couronne de petits bouquets, soit laissez apparent un bout du support en foin. Pliez le ruban en deux dans le sens de la longueur, puis nouez-le au milieu avec un bout de fil de fer dont vous accrocherez les extrémités à la couronne.

ALL BUNCHED UP

A hanging bunch of dried flowers, the interior design version of a posy, makes a charming wall decoration for any room in the home. This design was created for a young girl's bedroom, where it is displayed with a collection of Greek pottery.

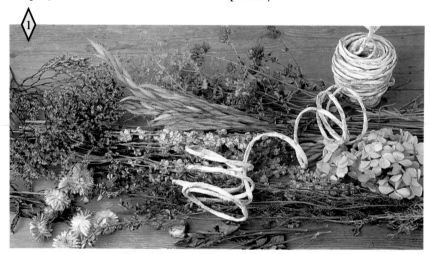

1 Make your selection of dried flowers in colours that will blend perfectly with the proposed site for the decoration. Those to be placed at the back of the bunch will need suitably long stems.

2 Compose the dried flower bunch flat on a table. Place the longest stems, in this case the grasses, so that they will fan out at the back of the arrangement. Cover them with blue larkspur, the tips widely spaced and the stems close together.

3 Arrange stems of pink larkspur over the blue ones. Position a few marjoram stems in the centre and shorter sprays of lady's mantle from side to side. Arrange a few pink roses in the centre, and then strawflowers at varying heights. Place short stems of sea lavender so they will fan out at the sides of the bunch.

4 Bind the stems with silver wire.
Before pulling the wire tight,
rearrange the stems until the shape is
pleasing. Tuck in a few short stems of
hydrangea.

5 Unfurl the length of paper ribbon
from each end but leave the centre
section tightly furled. Wrap the centre
section tightly around the stems and tie
in a knot. Tie the ends into a bow,
adjusting to make a full, rounded shape,
and cut the ends at a slant.

DÉCOR CAMPAGNARD

Il vous faut

Un large vase rond ou tout autre type de récipient ● Un bloc de mousse sèche ● De l'argile adhésive de fleuriste ● Des ciseaux ● Une soucoupe en plastique pour poser le bloc de mousse ● Du ruban adhésif de fleuriste étroit ● Un choix de fleurs séchées comprenant des pivoines, des immortelles à bractées et du safran ● Des capsules de pavots séchés ● Des tiges de feuilles séchées comme l'Elaeagnus ● Des feuilles conservées et des bractées comme l'eucalyptus et les campanules ● Des ciseaux de fleuriste.

Retrouvez dans votre maison les vibrantes couleurs et les formes variées des bordures de plantes herbacées dans cette composition qui capte les beautés de l'été. Elle comprend des fleurs, des feuilles et des bractées conservées dans la glycérine.

1 Les plantes ont été conservées suivant différentes méthodes. Les pivoines, les immortelles à bractées et les capsules de pavots ont été séchées en bottes, suspendues à l'air. Grâce à cette méthode, les pivoines ont gardé leurs longues tiges et leurs feuilles qui serviront de base au décor. Toutes les feuilles ont été séchées dans des cristaux de gel de silice dans un micro-ondes, et les bractées ont été mises dans une solution de glycérine et d'eau chaude.

2 Appliquez fortement la soucoupe en plastique destinée à recevoir la mousse sur le bloc de mousse pour qu'elle y laisse son empreinte. Retirez-la et découpez la mousse selon la forme du récipient. Coupez des bandes d'argile adhésive et placez-les sous la soucoupe. Placez-la sur le col du vase, puis déposez-y le bout de mousse découpé. Piquez de courtes gerbes de feuilles tout autour de la mousse. Plantez au centre trois longues tiges de campanules pour définir la hauteur de la composition, puis ajoutez des gerbes d'eucalyptus.

3 Répartissez les pivoines de manière à donner une forme ronde à la composition. Si les tiges ont été raccourcies et les feuilles enlevées, placez ces bottes en alternance avec les fleurs. Disposez les tiges courtes d'eucalyptus autour de la base du bouquet.

4 Mettez de courtes tiges de safran en bas du bouquet. Faites bien tout le tour du vase pour répartir régulièrement les feuilles et le safran de façon à dissimuler la mousse et son support.

5 Terminez la composition en ajoutant des tiges de safran plus hautes entre les pivoines. Ajoutez deux ou trois grosses capsules de pavot sur les côtés et de plus petites au centre en les enfonçant bien. Enfin, rajoutez quelques immortelles à bractées orange pour soutenir l'orange chaud du safran.

DUTCH INFLUENCE

You Will Need

urn-shaped container raised on a short foot ● piece of plastic-covered wire mesh netting ● narrow florists' adhesive tape ● scissors ● florists' scissors ● selection of dried flowers such as larkspur, statice, roses, rosebuds, strawflowers, lady's mantle, marjoram, hydrangea, and carnations ● long foliage

Inspired by the magnificent paintings of the Dutch Masters, this arrangement is composed in a painted and gilded wooden urn. A cluster of fruits – pineapple, grapes, and pomegranates – and a jug of rich ruby wine complete the luxurious quality of the still-life group.

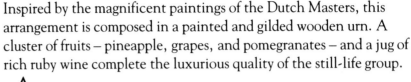

1 Choose a container with an interesting texture or colour combination, or paint one to harmonize with the room scheme and the flowers. Choose some long-stemmed flowers such as larkspur and air-dried roses to give the design height. If the flowers have been dried in the microwave, and have short stems, mount them on stub wires and bind with gutta percha (floral) tape.

2 Crumple the wire mesh netting and place it in the neck of the vase. Tuck in any stray ends. Cut short lengths of adhesive tape, twist them around the wire at intervals, and stick them to the rim of the container. When the design has been completed, the tape will be covered by the shortest of the flowers. Position the larkspur stems to create a fan shape.

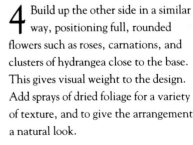

3 Build up one side of the design. Arrange the roses – here they are deep and pale pink and rich cream – among the larkspur stems. Cut the stems in graduated lengths, so that some roses are positioned close to the rim of the container.

4 Build up the other side in a similar way, positioning full, rounded flowers such as roses, carnations, and clusters of hydrangea close to the base. This gives visual weight to the design. Add sprays of dried foliage for a variety of texture, and to give the arrangement a natural look.

5 Complete the arrangement by filling in all the gaps with more and more dried flowers until it has a generous and opulent appearance. You may like to mount groups of hydrangea bracts on stub wires and use these for contrasting highlights.

BOUQUET DE MARIÉE

Le romantisme des roses, l'aspect flou des gypsophiles, le luxe des orchidées de Singapour, mélangées toutes ensemble en un bouquet porté par la mariée ou ses demoiselles d'honneur, resteront un souvenir éternel de ce jour merveilleux.

1 Choisissez des fleurs symbolisant le mariage. Ici le choix des couleurs va du mauve pastel des statices au violet profond des orchidées de Singapour, teintes rehaussées par du crème doux, du blanc et du vert pâle.

2 Coupez de courts bouquets de statices. Tigez-les avec du fil de fer, puis attachez-les avec du fil argenté. Entourez les tiges et le fil avec une bande serrée de gutta-percha. Faites de même pour les bractées d'hortensias, les gypsophiles et les roses à queues courtes.

3 Rassemblez naturellement en cascade différentes fleurs et feuillages. Recommencez jusqu'à obtenir une composition agréable, puis attachez l'ensemble avec du fil argenté.

4 Ajoutez des éléments au bouquet jusqu'à obtenir une forme parfaite. Alternez les formes rondes et pleines des roses et des immortelles à bractées avec les tiges des gypsophiles et des alchémilles. Attachez le bouquet avec un ruban, en le laissant filer jusqu'en bas.

5 Attachez le plus de ruban possible autour de la poignée de façon à créer de belles rosettes dont les extrémités traîneront. Ajustez les extrémités en les coupant en biseau ou en forme de V. Pour éviter d'abîmer les fleurs, mettez le bouquet dans un vase ou tout autre récipient jusqu'au jour du mariage. Si vous désirez le garder après le jour de la cérémonie, rangez-le à l'abri de la lumière.

BABY'S BOUQUET

The birth or baptism of a baby can be celebrated with a long-lasting floral gift. This design, which would be a delightful decoration for a nursery, is composed of a blend of dried flowers – sea lavender in two colours – and designer blooms in an open-work basket.

1 Select designer flowers as you would fresh ones, in colours that tone or harmonize and in a variety of shapes. Here, life-like hydrangeas were chosen to hold the centre of the design, with deep pink peonies, roses in a paler tint, and sprays of statice as a filler.

2 In an arrangement such as this, an open-work basket will reveal the stem-holding materials aiding the composition of the design. In an arrangement of all natural materials, lavender or thyme stems, or even sea lavender, could be woven in and out of the slats. As this basket may take pride of place among the nursery decorations, a toning pink paper ribbon was chosen instead. Unfurl the paper and thread it in and out, over and under each slat. Overlap the two ends at the back until the weaving is secure.

3 Cut two lengths of adhesive clay, press onto the underside of the prongs and press the prongs onto the base of the basket, one each side of the centre. Press the foam onto the prongs. Arrange sprays of sea lavender all around the foam to make a foundation for the designer flowers. Bend or cut the stem of one of the hydrangeas and place it at the centre back to define the height of the design.

4 Arrange the other hydrangeas, the peonies, and roses to make a dome shape, with the deep and pale pinks alternating. Fill in the spaces with designer statice. It is a matter of choice whether the artificial flower stems are cut – which requires wire cutters and a strong wrist – or bent so they can be used full length in another design. It is a question of choice, too, whether most or all of the leaves are discarded; they are usually far less realistic than the made flowers.

5 Fill in any spaces with sprays of sea lavender, which reinforce the 'natural' look of the display. Unfurl about 75cm (30in) of the paper ribbon and tie a bow. Fix the bow to the front of the basket with a piece of adhesive clay or a stub wire.

BLEU LAVANDE

L'odeur entêtante de la lavande est un élément incomparable pour fabriquer une couronne destinée à une chambre, à une salle de bain, au rebord d'une fenêtre, ou à un endroit où vous désirez apporter une pointe de romantisme. Une couronne plus petite peut être accrochée dans une armoire ou décorer un portemanteau.

1 Pour faire des petits bouquets s'alternant avec les bottes de lavande, choisissez des fleurs ayant des teintes douces et complémentaires, le bleu, le crème et le vert conviennent parfaitement. Si vous ne possédez pas de pistolet à colle, fixez les bottes et les petits bouquets à l'armature avec des bouts de fil de fer recourbés en forme d'agrafe.

2 Rassemblez environ huit ou dix tiges de lavande pour en faire un bouquet, coupez les queues court et attachez-les avec du fil argenté. Faites des petits bouquets mélangés – il y en a six dans cet exemple – avec les autres fleurs séchées, en disposant les fleurs rondes et pleines comme les roses et les bleuets au centre, et les gerbes plus élancées sur les côtés. Attachez les tiges avec du fil de fer.

3 Étalez une fine couche de colle le long des tiges de la première botte de lavande, puis pressez-la sur l'armature en la tenant fermement pendant quelques secondes pour que la colle prenne. Mettez ensuite de la colle sur les autres et fixez-les en faisant bien attention que toutes les têtes recouvrent les queues de la botte précédente. Faites ainsi le tour complet de la couronne en alternant la lavande et les petits bouquets suivant votre inspiration.

4 Coupez le ruban en six bandes égales. Faites un nœud avec chacune de ces bandes et taillez les extrémités. Coupez des bouts de fil de fer, puis pliez-les en U. Fixez cinq des nœuds à l'intérieur de la couronne et un sur le dessus. Collez des têtes d'immortelles à bractées pour dissimuler les trous et les bouts de fil argenté.

5 Ajustez les nœuds avec soin. Accrochez la couronne au mur, posez la sur une table ou encore dans une boîte dont le fond est recouvert de lin.

SUMMER CASUAL

You Will Need

straw hat with wide brim ● thick wire to encircle the brim ● selection of dried flowers such as peonies, sea lavender, and rosebuds ● dried leaves such as purple sage ● dried poppy seedheads ● 4cm- (1½in-) wide ribbon such as checked gingham ● scissors ● roll of florists' silver wire ● florists' scissors ● half a stub wire

Decorated with peonies and tied with pink and white gingham ribbons, this is a hat for the young at heart. Wear it on a summer picnic, or for an informal lunch in the garden. The very young could even wear this stylish and pretty hat to a country wedding.

1 Cut a piece of thick wire long enough to encircle the hat brim, and bend a hook into each end to make it easier to slip on and off the hat. Choose a ribbon in colours that tone with the flowers.

2 Cut a length of ribbon long enough to cover the wire circle, allowing a little extra to turn under the wire. Turn under one end to neaten it, wrap the ribbon close to the hook on one end of the wire and bind it in place with silver roll wire. Ease the ribbon around the wire circle, turn in the other end and bind it close to the second hook. Gather the dried flowers into four posies, with a peony, a rosebud, and a poppy seedhead in each. Cut the stems short and bind them with silver roll wire. Bind the first posy onto the ribbon-covered wire circle.

3 Bind on the remaining three flower posies so the heads of each successive one cover and conceal the stems of the one before. The design will have the appearance of a continuous ribbon of flowers. When the decoration is in place, slip the ribbon band over the hat and fasten the two hooks.

4 Make a bow from more ribbon and leave trailing ends. Bend half a stub wire to make a U-shaped staple, push it through the loop at the back of the bow and push the ends through the hat. Bend them back so they are flat against the inside of the crown.

5 Perfect for any casual summer occasion – several flower-decked hatbands can be made in a range of colours to fit any plain straw hat.

MAGIE DES PÉTALES

Ce récipient rectangulaire en verre va être rempli d'un pot-pourri rose vif. Un morceau de mousse sèche servira de pique-fleurs, supportant une sélection de fleurs séchées du jardin et d'herbes qui seront réparties telles qu'elles poussent naturellement.

1 Sélectionnez un pot-pourri dont les couleurs se mélangent bien avec les fleurs séchées choisies pour la composition. Celle-ci comprend un mélange de pétales de roses et d'œillets roses et jaunes. Pour obtenir un meilleur effet, incluez des fleurs de grande taille, des pivoines et des œillets dans notre exemple, pour donner à la composition de la profondeur et son aspect tacheté.

2 Coupez deux bandes d'argile adhésive, collez-les sous les pique-mousse en plastique que vous poserez au fond du récipient. Taillez le bloc de mousse pour qu'il puisse rentrer dans le récipient, en prenant soin de laisser un espace de 1,5 cm tout autour et qu'il dépasse de 2,5 cm. Fixez la mousse sur les pique-mousse en plastique en effectuant une légère pression. Remplissez toutes les faces du récipient de pot-pourri à l'aide d'une cuillère en montant jusqu'en haut de la mousse.

3 Commencez la composition en disposant des plantes de manière légère et espacée, comme de la marjolaine pâle et mauve sombre qui est utilisée ici. Coupez certaines des tiges très court et placez-les de façon à ce que les fleurs jaillissent. Il est important que la composition ait du volume, de la profondeur et surtout soit à l'avant du récipient.

4 Arrange the rosebuds at intervals through the design to follow the outline of the marjoram. Position some of the largest of the dried flowers – carnations and peonies – low at the front, with some flower heads overlapping the container rim. Arrange a fan shape of statice extending to each side of the design, cutting short the stems to be positioned at the front.

5 Fill in the design with the fluffy green and yellow stems of the lady's mantle – the very essence of a cottage garden. Gather the cornflowers into bunches and position them – the brightest blooms in the arrangement – in clusters. Check that the rim of foam is completely hidden by the flowers placed at the sides of the arrangement. Turn the container around and complete the reverse of the design.

A BATHROOM COVER-UP

A dried-flower arrangement may seem paradoxical in a hot and steamy bathroom – but not if it is under permanent protection. This design, a modern version of a Victorian flower dome, is created on the pine base of a cheese dish and covered with the clear glass lid.

1 Select dried flowers in sharply contrasting colours so they do not blend into an unidentifiable mass when covered with the glass dome or lid. Blue, white, and yellow statice; yellow helichrysum, lady's mantle, and rosebuds; and blue cornflowers were used in this design.

2 Press a small strip of adhesive clay to the base of the plastic prong and press it onto the centre of the base. Cut the foam to the size and shape required and press it onto the prong. Arrange a ring of white statice around the base, the stems placed horizontally in the foam. Make a dome shape with yellow rosebuds. Put on the glass cover to check that the stems are not too tall.

3 Arrange short stems of blue and yellow statice between the rosebuds and then, to soften the effect, add short sprays of helichrysum and lady's mantle.

4 Position cornflowers evenly throughout the design. Turn the base around and check that it is equally well covered from every angle.

5 Once the cover is in place the dried flowers are well protected from any steam. To make a complete seal, press a narrow strip of modelling clay such as Plasticine all around the rim of the base and scatter a few highly-absorbent silica gel crystals among the dried flowers. Then press the cover onto the clay to complete the seal.

EASTERN RICHES

You Will Need

deep, round earthenware container;
a flowerpot or jug would be suitable
* *piece of florists' wire mesh netting*
* *narrow florists' adhesive tape*
* *scissors* • *florists' scissors*
* *secateurs (pruning shears)*
* *selection of dried flowers and*
seedheads such as shumag, caspia,
nigella Orient, bottle brush, and
amaranthus; pine and fir cones
could also be included.

Capture the spirit of the East with an arrangement of exotic dried flowers and seedheads in rich glowing reds, woody browns, and subtle greens. The rough earthenware container, a traditional yogurt pot, is the centre of a collection of pottery gathered on holiday travels.

1 Choose dried materials varied in both texture and colour, and include some types with the look of intricately carved wooden flowers. Some florists sell bags of assorted materials simply labelled 'exotics'. If these are available, some of the flowers and seedheads will have to be mounted on stub-wire stems.

2 Crumple the wire mesh netting to fit into the neck of the container. Criss-cross two strips of adhesive tape over the mound of wire netting and press the ends to the rim of the container. Begin the design by placing some of the tallest stems in a fan shape. Cut some of the stems so that the height is graduated.

3 Fill in the design with some of the more solid shapes, grouping them together in twos and threes to maximize their impact. Place some stems so they dip over the rim of the container.

4 Remember that red and green are colours that complement each other, and position some of the red feathery flowers to nestle among the flattering green materials.

5 Complete the design by positioning some of the cone-like seedheads to cover the container rim while others provide the contrast of full, round shapes.

BRIGHT PERSONALITY

An old brass watering-can, burnished until it shines, holds a riot of colourful materials. Some glow with their natural hues and others – the poppy seedheads, sprays of preserved and bleached leaves, and miniature thistles – have been dyed to coordinating shades. This is a perfect design for a sun-room or conservatory, fireplace, or porch.

1 Chinese lanterns (winter cherry), the most vibrant of all seed carriers, give this design its colour impact. The purple seedheads provide a muted but striking contrast, and the bleached and dyed foliage link the two elements. A few spiky green leaves, dried in the microwave, break the two-colour monopoly.

2 Crumple the wire netting and fit into the neck of the container. Anchor it with two or three short lengths of adhesive tape wrapped around a strand of wire and stuck onto the container rim. Arrange the foliage to make a fan shape with the tallest stems in the centre and the shortest ones at the side.

3 Cut the stems of the dyed poppy seedheads to varying lengths and arrange them in clusters, with some extending well beyond the side of the container. Handle the material carefully – the dark-coloured dye may stain fingers or clothing.

4 Arrange the smaller plant material – the spiky dyed thistles – in tight clusters, grouping short stems close around the rim of the container, where they will conceal the crumpled wire.

5 Repeat the fan shape of the bleached leaves, poppy seedheads and thistles on the other side of the container, angling some stems almost horizontally into the crumpled wire mesh. Distribute stems of the orange Chinese lanterns (winter cherry) evenly through the design, with some dipping low over the container, caught in its reflection.

SCENTED RING

A preformed ring covered with colourful and fragrant potpourri and decorated with a dried flower posy makes a romantic design for a bedroom, and a charming gift for family and friends of all ages.

1 You could use a dry foam ring in place of the stem ring, but it does not have the same aesthetic appeal in such a pretty decoration. Choose potpourri in colours to complement the chosen room scheme, or in the favourite colours of the recipient.

2 Hot glue gives the most quick and easy results, but a clear all-purpose glue may be used instead. Spurt the glue onto the ring a little at a time, and press the potpourri onto it. Take care not to burn your fingers when using hot glue. Allow to cool for a few seconds before pressing on the petals.

3 Work all around the ring, gluing and pressing on the petals until the form is covered on top, both inside and outside. If there are any gaps, spurt on a little more glue and add more petals. Glue some of the most colourful petals on top to give the ring a bright appearance.

4 Arrange the dried flowers to make a small posy. Cut short the stems and bind them with silver wire. Bend the stub wire in half to make a U-shape, loop it over the stems and press the ends of the wire into the ring, to secure the posy on top.

5 Tie the ribbon around the ring form, bringing the ends over the top, where they will cover the posy stems and binding wire. Tie the ribbon into a bow and trim the ends neatly.

Note
Place the ring away from strong light. If it fades and loses some of its fragrance, glue on a few more petals and sprinkle the decoration – but not the ribbon – with a few drops of potpourri oil, or an essential oil such as neroli.

WINTER GARDEN

Think of a field of wheat at twilight; think of the dramatic shapes of seedheads as they dry in the flower borders; think of the excitement of coming across a patch of wild mushrooms in a meadow – and bring all those elements together in an unusual composition of contrasting plant materials.

1 This design features plant materials found in the wild, and others with dramatic rather than delicate shapes. To dry fungi, place on a rack in the oven for several hours at the lowest temperature, or leave for several days in a warm, dry place, such as an airing cupboard or boiler room.

2 Cut the foam block into pieces that will fit tightly into the container. The foam should come to within about 2cm (¾in) of the top of the basket. It is not necessary to use any holding or fixing materials. Cover the foam with moss so that it comes just above the basket rim.

3 Cut the stub wires in half and push a wire into the stalk of each of the dried mushrooms. Arrange the mushrooms in a group at one corner of the basket, some on short stalks overlapping the rim and others standing tall.

4 Press short-cut stalks of carthamus into the foam close to the mushrooms. Position poppy seedheads, their stalks cut to uneven lengths, in a group behind the fungi.

5 Add taller stems of the orange carthamus to form a group. Create a patch of wheat in the corner opposite the fungi, and position short stalks of dried thistle to add to the textural interest. Use stub wires to 'tease' the moss between the stalks and ensure that there are no tell-tale signs of stem-holding foam.

PRESSED INTO SERVICE

A ring of pressed autumn leaves and dried seed carriers makes an unusual and highly-textured wall decoration. To protect the plant materials, place them behind glass in a frame, mount them on coloured cardboard and cover with transparent film, or display them under the glass top of a coffee table.

1 Draw the inner and outer rims of the ring on the cardboard, and cut it out. This design is 28cm (11in) diameter. Make the selection of pressed leaves as varied as possible in both shape and colour.

2 Put small dabs of glue onto the tip, centre, and stem end of each leaf and arrange them, overlapping, so the tips extend beyond the inner and outer rims of the cardboard ring. Cover the leaves with a sheet of plain paper and press firmly with your hand. Put dabs of glue at intervals on the back of a large and shapely leaf, place this onto the first layer, and press it in place.

3 Continue to build up layers of leaves and seed carriers so that the design is full of interest and contrast.

4 The completed ring, an interpretation of a carpet of fallen leaves in a woodland, looks best mounted on colours in keeping with the autumnal theme. Choose muted greens, rich creams, clear greys, and burnt umber in preference to strong or primary colours which may overshadow the subtle colour blend of the leaves.

INDEX

Step-by-step projects are written in *italic*.